THE ALL TERRAIN CEO

LESSONS FOR LEADING TURNAROUNDS ACROSS THE WORLD

© Pascal Wuillaume, 2024
Website: pascalwuillaume.com

Author: Pascal Wuillaume
Title: CEO ALL-TERRAIN

ISBN: 979-87-010-9109-0

Second edition.
All translation, reproduction and adaptation rights reserved for all
countries.

Layout: bvg.studio

PASCAL WUILLAUME

THE ALL TERRAIN CEO
LESSONS FOR LEADING TURNAROUNDS ACROSS THE WORLD

The use of the masculine is only intended to lighten the text and identify without discrimination, individuals of both sexes.

Contents

To my children Alexis and Laetitia;

To my son-in-law Nicolas;

To my grandchildren Octave and Lucie and Emile;

To my ex-wife Aline who has encouraged me throughout my professional career;

To Michel, Daniela, Ute, Etienne, Miha, Enguerrand, Jean-Pierre, Dries, Eleonore, Kathryn and Catherine, who thanks to their inspiration, their help and patience made the writing of this book possible.

Foreword

The more exceptional a work, the shorter its foreword.

This has been the case for centuries with remarkable texts which have not had to bother with any prior recognition.

This preface will not be - as it often is with the secondary opus - a foreword of convenience, but rather a testimony to the intelligence and the pen of the author.

This book is not a primer on professional codes, but rather a set of advice and wise thoughts for a happy, fulfilling career that is built in an informed and humanistic way.

What are the first words that came to my mind after reading the manuscript? The need for resilience, the need to balance choices, intellectual and managerial flexibility, the wise development of intuition and the importance of empathic cooperation.

But there is a higher value that this book carries in the fabric of a CEO: character. It is a diffuse notion filled with rigor, solidity, and perseverance which Charles de Gaulle said was a virtue in difficult times.

This book is not to be put in everyone's hands, but in those of those who will have the intelligence to read, slowly and in reflection, the fabric of Pascal Wuillaume's thought.

It is enlightened and inspiring. But make no mistake: it also carries the requirement of a life discipline.

And finally, combining my own professional experience with that of Pascal Wuillaume, I will conclude by saying that an ancestral principle must animate the action of a leader: the humility of the person and the greatness of the task.

Prof. Dr. Bruno Colmant
Member of the Royal Academy of Sciences,
Letters and Fine Arts of Belgium

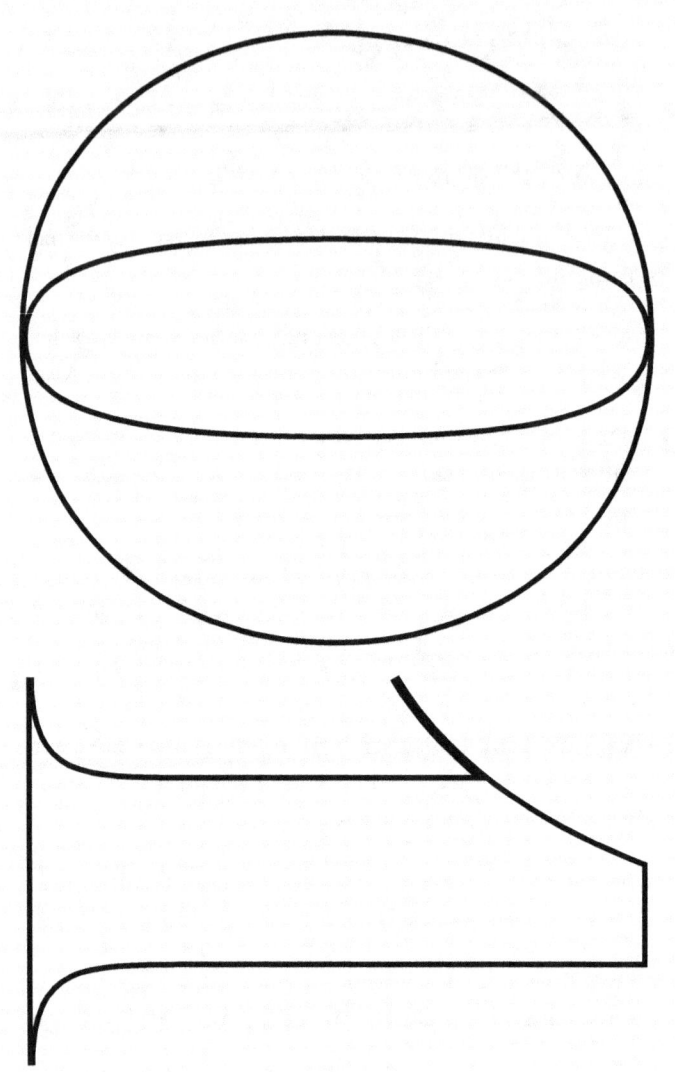

MY PERSONAL AND HUMAN EXPERIENCE

I'm on a plane. A Boeing 747. JFK Airport isn't far away. Manhattan is below and the plane flies over it. I left Paris. I left Brussels, I left Ghent. At not yet 30, I am leaving Europe. From my past, I only keep 2 suitcases with me and also a 1 m³ container full of my personal items. My future is ahead of me. New York. Life awaits me. The world is waiting for me. Everything is still to be accomplished, invented, dared.

CHAPTER 1
Expatriation

Why choose the right company before your 30s?

I was a consultant at AC Nielsen in Brussels. My job was super interesting, and I was making a good living. However, a voice inside repeatedly said: "I want to discover the world!"

That year, during the summer vacation, windsurfing on a lake in the Netherlands, I made my decision. It was clear. If the opportunity ever presented itself, I would join a large international company that could give me the opportunity to work internationally. And as always, when all the radars are pointed toward the same goal, things come to you. A few weeks later, I mentioned my wish to a cousin living in Paris. He worked for a large French IT group. Within a week, I received a call for an interview. After a few months, I was hired as a sales engineer in Lille at Honeywell-Bull, in charge of the hospital sector in the region. Two years later, I was promoted to New York and after five years I left that beautiful city to take over the general management of Bull Far East in Singapore.

What do I remember from all that?

First of all, I chose the right company. In Belgium, there were many great opportunities, but often in small subsidiaries of international groups. Joining a French group which, at the time, had a turnover equivalent to 10 billion euros today, which employed 40,000 people and which was present in more than 60 countries, provided me with a multitude of opportunities for an international career.

How does performance make the difference?

During the first two years, I had no contact with the group's international network; all my energy was focused on the success of my commercial activities in my sector. I believe I visited all the hospitals in the region several times and installed their first computers in most of them. However, a computer and its installation at the time cost over a million euros. We were a team of four sales engineers, assisted by several technical engineers. There was a tremendous emulation between us and a great understanding. After two years of collaboration, and with a remarkable district manager, our team was considered to be the most successful north of Paris. This gave us visibility within the group.

The first condition for advancing in your career is, of course, to be successful in your current job!

How to move out of your cocoon?

In the IT sector, there were many new developments, as well as product launch meetings at the group's headquarters in Paris. This allowed me to meet a lot of people in various jobs (marketing, finance, R&D, HR), to make friends but also to make connections outside of my immediate network.

At that time, Paris hosted an annual trade fair for office automation, IT, networks and telecommunications (the SICOB). Salespeople were invited to lend a hand at the Honeywell-Bull booth. So, every year at the beginning of October, I inevitably spent 10 days working on the group's stand.

If you are an executive in a group and if you have the possibility, take the opportunity to be trained, to participate in product launch events and offer to be part of working groups. All of this participation will help you move out of your cocoon.

What do you really want in life?

It was in 1985, at SICOB, that my big international step took place. In August I'd visited my parents in Chicago where my father was working. Upon my return to Lille, I said to myself: "Pascal, if you stay here, you will die ...".

I therefore took advantage of being at SICOB to meet clients but above all to meet informally with the group's HR manager in charge of international business. I told him that my wish was to work for an affiliate abroad. Then the opportunity came: a sales position had just opened in New York in the Honeywell network to handle projects in Europe and Africa for Fortune 500 companies, the UNDP, and the World Bank. There were thirty candidates for the position. My good past performance and hitting it off with my possible future boss Yves L. around a seafood platter in a Parisian restaurant did the trick...

So never be afraid to make inquiries around you. Opportunities will come one day. However, before expressing your request, be clear with yourself about what you want, your motivations and the possible consequences of your choices.

How do you think your boss will react?

To be honest, the big boss in charge of the network north of Paris was not at all pleased, even furious, to learn that I had been chosen for the New York position by the International Business department. He summoned me to Paris to persuade me to stay. He told me that more opportunities would come one day. I held firm and life proved me right. In the wake of the rapid evolution of the IT world, I was the last Belgian to hold this position.

I remember, when I was CEO, the challenges I had to face the spontaneous agreement of managers for releasing one of their subordinates for joining a group project team.

What are the right attitudes and skills?

Let's be honest, not everyone has the right skills to work internationally. Thanks to the European ERASMUS and other exchange programs, millions of European students can now experience life in other cultures. My daughter Laetitia had the opportunity to do a summer internship in the USA and to take courses during several six-month stays in Mexico and India.

So, I encourage all parents to inspire their children to take advantage of these unique opportunities that study abroad scholarships offer. This allows each young person to gain self-confidence and to better understand other cultures, outside their country.

However, the first skill you need to have, if you want to work abroad, is a perfect mastery of the local language. You will have to liaise with customers, prepare offers, give conferences, manage teams in their mother tongue. A notable exception are Asian countries where it is customary to communicate in English if you are a foreigner.

The second skill you need to have, is to master your job. I remember back then there were French people at the Honeywell plant in Phoenix, but they were all very skilled engineers in their respective fields. As a salesperson, my only possibility was to find a position in the group's sales network. It is therefore illusory to think that a company will send you abroad for a position for which you do not have the required skills. Certain professions are more suitable for international transfers such as engineers, people in finance, consultants or buyers.

The third skill to have is your ability to manage teams. Personally, I hadn't had the chance to prepare myself to be a manager. At 34 years old, I found myself in Singapore as the boss of general managers based in China, Indonesia, Malaysia and Thailand, not to mention New Caledonia and Tahiti. These men were all older than me. In Singapore I was in charge of the team, so I was even more handicapped: first, given my lack of management experience, and, above all, because I was very young for this position. My great strength laid in my energy and the easy contact I had with clients and prospects ...

Being a manager is a job that can be learned with some practice, although some coaching can really make the difference. Personally, I didn't have that chance. So do not hesitate, the day you are promoted, to ask the help of a coach. It is always beneficial to have somebody give you advice and help you avoid making beginner's mistakes.

What about family in all of this?

When we left Brussels, we first lived in Paris, where I was trained before moving to Lille. At that time, my wife worked at the Museum of Fine Arts in Brussels. So, she had to quit her job in order to follow me on my international journey.

Then our two children arrived, Alexis in Lille and Laetitia in New York. When we returned to Belgium almost 15 years later, my wife did not return to work.

Today, in most married couples, both people work. Most of the time, they each have a job that they enjoy. The discussion of going abroad must therefore take place almost before the marriage! The good news is that you no longer need a work permit inside the European Union. This considerably increases the chances for the partner (man or woman) to find a job in his field in another country. It is also possible to take unpaid leave when working for a large group. A good piece of advice anyway: don't wait until the last minute to raise the subject between yourselves.

The other good news is that all of the spouses we knew in New York and Singapore all easily resumed their professional careers upon returning home.

As my children were born when we were abroad, they attended international schools from their early childhood. When they grew up, they realized that it was difficult to leave their friends. I remember my kids saying: "Dad, every time we move, we lose our friends. At least when we visit Belgium during our vacation, our cousins are still there!" This is probably one of the reasons why my children have remained very attached to their large family to this day.

Another good thing was that we returned to Belgium when our children were old enough to enter secondary school. They therefore lived their teenage years in a stable family and school environment. They were able to create strong friendships that still last today. When we lived in Singapore, I remember seeing too many expat children around us who, by the time they were teenagers, felt confused and in great psychological distress.

I therefore suggest, if you have teenage children, that you respect their wishes if ever you have to expatriate yourself. A solution can usually be found.

What kind of state of mind for the big departure?

All my life I will remember that unique moment when my plane, approached JFK Airport and circled around Manhattan before landing a few minutes later. During those few moments, I realized that I had left everything in Europe. I was only able to take two suitcases and 1 cubic meter of personal items. I had let go of everything I had known for 29 years: my family, my friends, my world. Fortunately, my wife was going to arrive sometime later with our baby Alexis ...

For a few moments I felt a mix of fear and excitement. Sentences jumbled in my head: *"Will I be up to my new job?"* Waoow, I'm coming to New York! *"If I can make it there, I can make it anywhere!"*

I was fortunate at the time to receive a settling-in allowance from my company. I believe that is no longer the norm today.

The advice I can give you is to make your material life as easy as possible. You are expected to be operational: immediately. Your personal problems do not concern your company. So, I seeked help from a real estate agency to find a rental house in Larchmont, a stone's throw from the train station. I bought a car, a bed, a sofa. I contacted the local expat organization which provided me with all the good addresses. At the weekends, I visited garage and tag sales, and, in no time, we had our home. I could therefore devote myself body and soul to my professional duties.

How to reconcile expatriation and family life?

Every expatriate is sent by headquarters for a specific reason. One thing that all expats I have known have in common, is that they identify themselves with the group they represent. When we introduced ourselves among expatriates, we did not give our last name but the name of the company we worked for.

As an expat, I worked a lot. The burden of this task also took its toll on my family life, especially in Singapore. I travelled frequently to all my affiliates in the region. One evening, a neighbor said to me: "You know Pascal, your son waited for you outside all evening and then he finally came home when we told him you weren't coming ...". These are sentences that bring you to order and make you say: Stop! I have to organize myself differently. Years later, when I was CEO of a large press company in Belgium, without realizing it, I was once again in the process of shifting to work, work, work. I remember back then; a team of consultants were helping me for a turnaround of the company. One day, Michel V. gave me this advice: "You know Pascal, you should arrange your schedule with fixed times for your exercise, your wife, your children, cultural outings, etc.". I don't know if my kids noticed it, but I remember putting this system in place to make time for what is most important in my life: my family.

What are the benefits of expatriation?

As far as I am concerned, being an expat propelled me to new heights in terms of responsibilities at a young age. I have spoken with others with similar experiences and all have had the opportunity for far greater responsibilities away from headquarters than if they had remained in their own country.

What we all have in common is managerial responsibility. When you arrive in a subsidiary, sent by head office, you are immediately faced with a managerial job. What's more, we are alone to confront specific situations, far from headquarters and all its support teams. There are a lot of things we have to deal with that most of our colleagues will never know about. Renegotiating office rents, talking to banks and local governments, dealing with staff demands, making sure bills are paid, etc.; therefore, very early in your career, you are faced with situations that most of your former colleagues at headquarters will never experience.

Another factor is the size of the affiliate you manage. It's not just about managing a budget with goals to achieve and doing it with a small team. Suddenly, you are faced with a turnover of tens of millions of dollars, with margins and costs to be respected, with all the associated complexities.

That said, the day you submit your resume, you will never have to justify your ability to manage a team and a large turnover. You will be one step ahead of your peers.

How not to be forgotten

All is not bright in the land of the rising sun ... You are far away. There is a time difference. You live in a different environment with radio, television, the local press broadcasting news that has nothing to do with the country from which you are from. And so, little by little, as the saying goes: "Out of sight, out of mind". You distance yourself from other members of your group, but also from your professional network, headhunters, etc.

Fortunately, in 2021 we have some fantastic communication tools. You have LinkedIn to keep in touch with your professional network, and Facebook, Instagram and other platforms like Zoom to stay in touch with family and friends.

My advice for those who have a mission far from home and who will therefore inevitably return one day, is to keep in touch! Contact headhunters regularly to let them know where you are. Force yourself to spend a few minutes on LinkedIn every day to keep in touch with your connections.

You never know what may happen. One thing is certain, the day you return home, no one will have waited for you in your company. Things will have evolved without you realizing it. There will have been reorganizations. Your former colleagues will no longer be in the same place or will have left the company. In short, if you are not careful, you will lose the "network" you built before you left. And so, sound advice from a friend: *Stay connected*!

I am in a good position to know this, having moved several times to various countries. I returned to Belgium in September 1995 as CEO of PCB (currently Pharma Belgium) and I had to restart my network from scratch. All around me, I had childhood friends who had made good progress in their professional lives and who had their own connections. Fortunately, my friends quickly introduced me to their networks. One positive thing that I learned when starting from scratch in an industry is to very quickly build a network. I love arriving at a cocktail party where I hardly know anyone and leaving with 10 new contacts. It has become a natural thing for me, and it helps me immensely in my new job as a consultant. Even COVID-19 was no excuse not to connect new professional contacts.

What are the advantages and disadvantages of time zones?

For 5 years, I worked in a time zone that was 6 hours behind Europe. When it was 9 a.m. in New York City, it was already 3 p.m. in Paris. Contrary to what one might think, this time difference really shortened response times. At the time, I often expected answers to technical, marketing and other questions from Paris. When I wrote to my colleagues at 6 p.m., the reply email had already arrived on my PC at 9 a.m. the next day. Another advantage was that at 1 p.m. my boss and I would go to lunch without being disturbed by our colleagues at headquarters. When I was in Singapore, it was the other way around: when Europe started its day at 9 a.m., it was already 3 p.m. But, in both cases, this time difference helped us to work faster with our international teams. On the other hand, during the short time in Singapore when I was reporting to Boston, the 12-hour time difference really weighed on my work as I had to adjust to Boston's schedule. So, when it was 9 a.m. in Boston, it was already 9 p.m. in Singapore … I'm not counting the number of conference calls I had at two in the morning … Not fun!

How to manage your assets from abroad?

During all my years of expatriation, the company paid for my rent, my car, my children's education and all medical expenses. It was therefore not too difficult to save a good chunk of my salary. However, I remember that at the end of the 1980s we experienced a boom in real estate in Belgium. All my friends who had invested in the housing sector at that time succeeded in creating a nice real-estate asset with a much lower income than mine. Indeed, you had to be there to "do good business".

Currently, even with the tools available online, the problem remains the same: you are far from "home". The advice I will give you, therefore, is to call on a financial advisor in your country of origin, who can manage your stock portfolio; a real estate advisor who can manage the possible purchase of a property in your absence. The main reason is fiscal. Back in the day, in the US, you were taxed 30% on your stock market gains, but you could deduct your losses. As of today, in Belgium, there is still no tax on stock market gains. Real estate taxation was also very different compared to European countries. Anyone who knows that he will return home one day should think about building his wealth according to the tax rules in place in his country of origin.

How to organize your return

In my case, the return home did not go as planned. At the time, although the Bull group bought out Honeywell's IT business, the English and Italian subsidiaries still reported to Boston and not to Paris. A reorganization of the group was decided, and these two countries were "given" to head office. In compensation, since they already managed Japan, the Americans received the management of the rest of Asia. A few months later, I received a call from Boston saying, "Pascal, I am moving to Singapore and I am taking your job". It was the biggest cold shower of my life! I had a dream job and we lived in a dream place. All of Asia was waking up and the opportunities there were immense. In addition, I was making a very good living.

I had to return to Europe without any psychological preparation, without a career plan, without a school for my kids. I found myself in an apartment hotel in the center of Paris with 7 suitcases and a container full of my belongings on the way to Le Havre. I remember that my children found it great fun living in Paris. Unlike many other expats, I did not originate from there, so I did not have my family cocoon, nor my inner circle of friends to support me during these difficult months. I quickly found a mission within the group, but the beat was gone. A year later, I took advantage of a voluntary departure: I left the group and the IT sector to find myself as international director at Chaffoteaux, a wall-hung gas boiler company. A chapter of ten years of hectic life in a rapidly changing industry had been turned.

I am telling you this story which is surely not unique. Before leaving, make sure you have something to fall back on when you go abroad. I assure you that no one is waiting for you on your return. Of course, you will have acquired great management experience, but you are no longer directly "usable" in a position in which you can show your know-how.

Personally, it took me a year to recover from this situation. Leaving my company and the IT business gave me the opportunity to go back to the drawing board.

I therefore do not regret this expat journey because it allowed me not only to experience incredible moments but also to discover the vastness of the world in which we live. I became a different man, and my children were able, from an early age on, to be citizens of the world. Isn't that the best gift I could possibly give them?

CHAPTER 2
Studies and continuing education

The importance of studies

For me studying has been a lesson of life. I thank my parents for enrolling me at the time in the best college in Ghent. Although there has been quite a bit of controversy on the subject, I am proud to have been educated in a Jesuit college. I still remember the compositions in which it was necessary to tirelessly include a thesis, an antithesis and a synthesis. The surprising and eclectic erudition of some teachers also opened my eyes to unknown worlds. My studies gave me a critical mind and opened me to knowledge. They were also a lesson in discipline. This school of life taught me to have a purpose in life and to find the courage to achieve it. So don't hesitate, dear parents, to choose the best school that is suitable for your children. You'll never regret it.

The choice of higher education

When I had to choose which subject I was going to study, my decision was quickly made after an information evening organized by the Department of Economics at the University of Antwerp. I was fortunate to study in a different city than mine, at a high-level university with exciting courses.

We all have skills and dreams! It is therefore very important to make the right choice of studies that will lead you towards your professional goal. I am amazed to hear today from friends of my generation - and even younger ones - who followed a path of study by choosing a branch "to please their parents" and who afterwards did the job that they wanted. What courage on their part not to have followed a career path just to please their parents. But at the same time, what a waste! They start their professional life after all with a handicap.

Many years later, when I was working in New York and made the decision to do an MBA, I hesitated between a regular university and a more prestigious one. My American assistant at that time, Kathy B., once said to me when I was hesitant: "Pascal, are you crazy? Just take the best and leave the rest!" I owe her a debt of gratitude for choosing NYU which is one of the world's top universities.

Many years later, I feel that making the right choices in my studies made my life easier: I feel rewarded every day for never having taken the easy road. Best of all, thanks to the Alumni programs I attended, I made new friends all over the world.

My first conclusions

— Learn to learn

What I have learned the most in life is to be a lifelong learner. I don't have that knot in my stomach anymore if I have to dive into an area I don't know, because I know that in a few months I will have learned the essential basics of the sector.

— Know how to summarize

I remember when I was working in New York, I learned one morning that my then CEO, Jacques S., was arriving via Concorde and was planning to visit a few American companies which were among our group's biggest clients in Europe. The management from Paris expected me to give them an "executive summary" of each client to visit and their business situation within our group. It all had to fit onto one page. It was then that I thanked my teachers who had trained us tirelessly on the importance of summarizing. Even today, I still immediately recognize someone who has this ability; there are so few of them. At each job interview, I ask the candidate to summarize his career in three minutes, even if it means going into further detail afterwards. Believe me, less than 5% of applicants succeed. If you want to become a CEO one day, learn how to summarize!

— Distinguish the essential from the incidental

In addition to knowing how to summarize, it seems important to me to differentiate between the essential and the incidental. There are only 24 hours in a day, and if we are to have proper privacy and restful sleep, we must be able to work within a 12 hour work day. The difficulty is that the more you rise in the ranks and the more you manage complex cases, the more you are forced to make choices. Actually, the time you have to devote to your work remains the same. I hear a lot of people around me talking about burnout. I am neither a doctor nor a psychologist, but it is not by accident that, at least for the people I know, this often falls on people who want to do their job thoroughly and who are very meticulous.

So do the exercise with your email inbox one day. Try to work on the most important emails first and leave the others behind. Promise?

Now here is a little story about large pebbles.

— Large pebbles and time management

One day, a professor was invited to give a talk on time management at an international conference bringing together important CEOs. He had only been given 15 minutes in the day's busy schedule. He arrived on time and took his seat.

In front of more than 100 people, he took out a large jar; then, with a slow gesture, he placed inside, one by one, pebbles the size of tennis balls.

When the jar was full of pebbles, he turned to his audience and asked, "Is the jar full?" All answered without hesitation: "Yes" and he asked: "Really?"

So, he grabbed his leather bag to remove a bag of gravel which he emptied into the jar filling to the top. And he asked again: "Is the jar full?".

This time, the intelligent audience having understood the meaning of the demonstration, answered: "Probably not!" And he added: "Good!"

Again he grabbed his leather bag and removed a bag of sand which he emptied into the jar and asked: "Is the jar full?" "No!" All the participants answered heartily.

"Good!" The old professor said with a touch of malice. He then grabbed the flask of water on the conference table and poured the water up to the top of the jar.

Then he asked the question: "What did I want to show you through this experiment?"

Someone raised his hand and replied, "You have just shown us that, although our schedule already seems very full, we can still try to fill it in order to be more efficient."

The professor then said: "This is not what I wanted to demonstrate. So, what did I demonstrate? Do you want to know?"

"What I wanted to show you is that if I had not placed the large pebbles first, I would never have been able to put everything else into the jar".

And the professor concluded:

"And you, in your life, what are your large pebbles? Your business, your family, making your dreams come true or something else? And what do you do with those large pebbles in your life?"

And to a thunderous applause, the professor left the room, raising a hand of thanks.

The large pebbles bring us back to our true values and to the place we really give them in the management of our time. I still have a paper diary next to my Outlook diary. This allows me to put things that I think are important first and bold. Then there will always be room for the rest. This story can also be applied to our life in general. Have I defined the large pebbles in my life? If so, am I honest with myself when I have to choose between two important dates, one private and the other professional?

The people who have worked with me are all familiar with the large pebble story.

The right time to do an MBA

A lot of people around me did their MBA right after graduating from college. Personally, I didn't see the point. Let's be honest, we all know that the subjects we learn during our studies are for the most part very theoretic. Real professional life starts with your first job and it is only after a few years that you finally land a really interesting job.

At that time, I did not yet have 10 years of professional experience. However, every time I met a senior executive in a major company, very often he was an MBA from a particular university. I then said to myself that if I wanted to grow in the upper levels and someday lead a company myself, it was a must. I had already learned a lot of things in my early professional years, but I felt that there was still so much that I hadn't yet mastered. If I really wanted to evolve, this path would be a unique opportunity for me to take the step.

The executive MBA

The difference between a normal MBA and an executive MBA, aside from the price, was that I could continue working, with classes held every Friday or Saturday for two years. These started in mid-August and ended in mid-July. Everything was done to make our life easier: the course material was purchased for us. We also had seminars organized over long weekends. Best of all, a study trip was planned in Japan.

The criteria for admission to the executive MBA program at New York University implied that one had to be a manager and have approximately 10 years professional experience, in addition to having excellent GMAT[1]results.

— The benefits

The first advantage is that I did not have to stop my job during these two years of study. The financial cost was very important despite the fact that my company paid 50%. By working, I continued to earn a living. I remember every Monday during those two years of school. Every weekend I was learning interesting things that I already wanted to put into practice when I got back to work. Whether in IT, marketing, finance, etc., I came back with innovative ideas to apply in the office. Unlike my college classes, what I learned was practical and applicable to my current job. Every Tuesday evening I had a meeting with 5 other students to

---

1. *The Graduate Management Admission Test (GMAT) is a standard test in English that measures skills deemed important for admission to an MBA program at a US university.*

work on the exercises due the following Saturday. I have fond memories of those evenings in our working group where we exchanged ideas. We learned to discover the "behind the scenes" of the other companies where the participants worked. It was through the eyes of my colleagues that I got a glimpse of what life was like inside General Electric and General Foods (now Kraft Foods).

— The disadvantages

Working and studying at the same time, plus traveling for business, took a heavy toll on my private and family life. This demanding time required a lot of sacrifice and effort on my part and on the part of my family. I thank them for their support.

I have great respect for people who didn't have the chance to go to school in their youth and who in their 30s decide to attend night school. I admire their courage and tenacity.

— The benefit justifies the cost

Finally, what did all this bring me? What changed the most in the way I think and work?

The first thing that comes to mind is that after graduation, I started to see things from a different perspective. It's as if I changed my orbit and I saw the whole earth and not just part of it. Whenever I had to analyse a case or solve a problem, I tried to see the big picture, in its complexity and especially in its ambiguity. Nothing is black or white. And as Jacques Brel said: *When you write a song, most of the words you use are in black and white, then you occasionally use one in colour. These coloured words are part of us because we give them meaning. If you wish, we give them a third dimension.* For me, it was about going more into the why of things, the why of the actions of certain people. To seek out the deep and often unconscious motivation behind things in life. To look for connections between things that appear different.

The second thing that comes to mind is self-confidence. I learned that anything can be learned and that there is no limit. I became fearless every time I started a new CEO job in a new company or a new industry.

The third and most obvious thing is the professional springboard this diploma provided me.

Continuing education

The world is constantly changing. The COVID-19 era has brought about a paradigm shift as do all disruptions. To believe that everything we learned in our youth is enough for the rest of our lives is a delusion. As CEO, we therefore need to question ourselves every day. That's why, especially for a CEO, it's worth spending one or two weeks a year attending a training or seminar in a specific focus area. It's a necessity, not a luxury. Now, how many leaders are doing this around you? We all have the same excuses: no time! ... and yet, paradoxically, what a time-saver and above all what a boost in energy and new ideas.

It was August 2020 when I received an email from my coach Etienne VDK who was organizing a "Get your business off the ground" seminar in the form of a three day online session. I had already taken this training in Barcelona in 2015 and it gave me a boost at the time. I was very curious to see how Etienne was going to succeed in this challenge via Zoom and that for three days. That summer, the COVID-19 crisis was in full swing. By attending this seminar in early September, I decided to start several new projects. Two months later, two of them had already been completed: the writing of a book on management, and my association within a private partnership focused on consulting and the implementation of business transformation projects.

Company training

A CEO owes his success above all to those around him. He has to make sure he surrounds himself with the best possible team. His role is also to identify talented young executives between 30 and 40 who have the potential to grow within his group. If nothing is planned for them, they will go to greener pastures. It is therefore important for any company of a certain size to have a pool of people who can be promoted one day. This pool is called HP or high-potential executives.

The high-potential executive

As a general rule, a manager is considered to be a High Potential if he can climb two hierarchical levels quickly enough from his current position and, in the longer term, if he can become a senior manager.

If you are between 30 and 40, what criteria should you meet to be considered as one of them?

* You must perform better than your peers and your skills must be noticed by your hierarchy.
* Your behaviour should reflect the culture and values of the company.
* You must have an open mind and a strong capacity to develop yourself.

Once you have defined a group of people within your group as HP, it is important to let them know and to create a specific training program for them. There are several companies specialized in this area to help you with this.

This continuous training of a few days per month or per quarter will provide the group with new essential skills needed for their future functions; these privileged sessions will also be the cement of a new cohesion between them.

CHAPTER 3
Know yourself and move forward with others

I never lose. Either I win or I learn

— *Nelson Mandela*

Mindset

If you want to move forward in life, you must dare to take risks, accept setbacks and above all, you must not believe that your path in life is defined from birth.

I often wondered what kind of essential ingredient I possess that has allowed me to run 7 companies in 7 different industries. What distinction made the difference? Why did I not have a simpler, more comfortable life with fewer moves and fewer job changes?

I finally discovered only recently what this essential element was. It happened while reading a cult book I'd heard about on an American billionaire's podcast. The book in question had changed the life of this man.

This book was called "Mindset" by Carol Dweck.

Her message is as follows: There are two types of personalities:

* Those who have a growth mindset
* Those who have a fixed mindset.

— A growth mindset

With a growth mindset, you believe that your qualities are primarily developed through your work. It doesn't matter where you start from because your personality, skills and competencies can develop over time. It's the effort that leads to success! You like to undertake projects, to take risks, to see your mistakes and failures as lessons in life. You are not afraid to show your weaknesses. You easily surround yourself with people who are more competent than you. In the end, you are happier, and you have a better chance of being successful in life.

Personally, since my early youth, I have always wanted to understand, learn and progress. Whenever I had a question, I consulted one of the 12 volumes of the Larousse encyclopaedia. Even today, my entourage blames me for always having my nose in Google and Wikipedia. I admit that I made a lot of mistakes during my first years as a manager, but this allowed me to better cope with the difficulties and challenges as a CEO of larger companies.

— A fixed mindset

With a fixed mindset, you believe that your qualities, your abilities and your personality are determined when you are born and cannot be changed. We are smart or not, we are good at maths or languages or not. You see your strengths and weaknesses as beliefs without being able to change anything. You will always try to confirm or prove your qualities and avoid taking risks. You often blame others for being the cause of your failures rather than taking responsibility and learning from your mistakes. You tend to take criticism badly, you take it as a personal attack.

I have to admit that I had moments of fixed mindset. I had accepted the position of CEO of AMP, a subsidiary of the Lagardère group, on condition that I could develop the Nordic countries in addition to Belgium. When I started my job, my mission was changed into the change management of the Belgian subsidiary. For two years, I was helped to succeed this mission by a PwC team led by Michel V. After three years, when I started to see some positive results, I asked for a meeting with the president of our division in Paris. I told him that I was unhappy that the assignment I was working on did not correspond to what had been agreed upon when I was hired. I might as well tell you that he didn't like my attitude. Six months later, I was thanked for my services, but with a beautiful golden parachute. I remember hearing him say, "Pascal, you do a good job, but you are not a good soldier".

It was only while reading this "Mindset" book last year that I realized that during this period of my life I had slipped into a fixed mindset. I did not realize that I was running a company with an updated turnover of over 800 million euros with 1,200 employees, that I had a unique opportunity to familiarize myself with the latest techniques of Business Transformation. If I had had a growth mindset back then I would have thanked my president for giving me this opportunity to surpass myself. This shock in my professional life forced me to foster a growth mindset and therefore to bounce back once more in my life.

And you? What mindset would you choose, to be successful and happy in life?

Knowledge and self-respect

As a small child, the only vision we have of ourselves is through the gaze of our parents. If parents encourage and give you confidence, you gain good confidence in your abilities and you will be more successful in life. In my case, I was the eldest son, third in a family of five, living in the region of Ghent. I had two French grandfathers who died before I was born. My Russian grandmother died when I was 9 years old. Unfortunately, I hardly knew my Belgian grandmother since she and my mother were not on speaking terms. The few memories I have from my childhood are linked to loneliness. I don't remember my mom or dad playing with me. In addition, we spoke French at home and in the street, the other children spoke a language that was foreign to me. So, we lived in a vacuum and it wasn't until the first year of primary school that I heard Flemish.

The image I had of myself was built up little by little through the eyes of others. From my teenage years and the years that followed, I made sure I was part of a lot of different groups. The important thing for me was to be accepted and respected. Meld myself into what is called the "establishment". This allowed me to be very comfortable thereafter in all types of societies in all the countries where I have travelled and lived.

It wasn't until much later in life that I began to realize that I deserved respect on my own; that the gaze of others was not that important. Everyone has a story and others also have their problems: they all see me through their own prism which is not mine. This is how humans work.

So, I hope you think about this. Do you feel deep inside that you respect yourself in all aspects of your life? This is an important question because it's only by respecting yourself that you can respect others. And respect for others is the basis of a good manager.

The judgment of others

Admit it: it's so easy to judge others. During all these years that I have had to lead and motivate teams, I have always had to deal with this dilemma.

When hiring an executive, I tried to put all the safeguards in place to ensure that the person I hired would be the ideal person for the job. In this mission, I was clearly in a state of judgment because the decision would have important consequences for the success or failure of my business plans.

Furthermore, having begun 7 times as a new CEO, with a management team in place, I especially had to refrain from judging my colleagues too quickly. I had to take the necessary steps to get to know them better. And so, throughout my life as a boss, I have faced this dilemma.

My advice to you is to try not to judge people too quickly. When in doubt, get to know them better. In hiring someone, you can get help from other people and share your thoughts. In other situations, you will be alone. So, take the necessary time before passing judgment on people or events.

Beliefs transmitted by our parents

Unconsciously, our parents and our ancestors, through them, transmitted beliefs in us. They can be supporting or limiting depending on whether they support a part of life or our entire existence. They can be limiting depending on whether they prevent us from evolving, choosing, feeling free…

Here are a few examples:

- ⊖ *Money does not bring happiness*
- ⊖ *Money is not what is important*
- ⊖ *I am not good enough to succeed*
- ⊖ *My chances of success are slim*
- ⊖ *Rich people are ungenerous people*
- ⊖ *I'm too young to ...*
- ⊖ *I'm too old to ...*
- ⊖ *Better to find a safe job*
- ⊖ *God will provide*
- ⊖ *Don't take too many risks!*
- ⊖ *Work on Sundays is forbidden!*
- ⊕ *I say what I do, and I do what I say*
- ⊕ *I have respect for myself and others*
- ⊕ *I do respect work*
- ⊕ *It is important to volunteer*
- ⊕ *It is important to be on time*
- ⊕ *It is important to keep your word*
- ⊕ *It is important to be honest*

I believe that if you want to be successful in life, it is important to get rid of all those phrases and thoughts that prevent you from moving forward and most importantly from being responsible for YOUR life. I call them blocking or limiting beliefs. For my part, when they do not suit me or do not suit me anymore, I put them aside. Or transform them by asking myself: What do I really want as an alternative?

For example, I used to believe *"Money does not bring happiness"*. I replaced it with *"Money brings me freedom"*. It's your turn ...

I remember an anecdote when I had just been appointed CEO of PCB (currently Pharma Belgium). I was living in Paris at the time and was driving towards Brussels to get to my new job. I received a phone call from my mother and in the conversation, she tells me: *"You know Pascal, it is not thanks to you that you have this position, but it is thanks to providence."* At the time, I didn't pay too much attention to that sentence.

Years later, at a psychological seminar in Germany, it came back to me and I was seized with an attack of rage. How could my own mother say this to me instead of congratulating me on all the hard work and effort that went into it? She had brushed aside with the back of her hand everything I had given of myself that had led to my appointment of this position, as if these efforts never existed, as if I never existed. Behind her phrase that "... it was just coming from heaven", she awakened in me what I had missed. A mother who helped me build my self-confidence. She was probably blinded by her own limiting beliefs and not available for the child that I was?

"The important thing is not what life has made of me but what I have done with it." Jump and move forward. Transform what happens to you and what has been given to you when it doesn't suit you anymore!

And you? What are your blocking beliefs? List them and make a solemn decision to throw them in the dustbin. Get rid of your heavy backpack and you will feel so much lighter and full of energy for a fresh start.

The attitude towards authority

Personally, I have always had a problem with authority.

For me, it was important to be able to admire my boss in order to respect him. If I had no admiration or if I found him less competent than me, I could not remain serene and I would enter into a latent or open conflict.

Once again, it was not until much later at a seminar in Germany that I realized that not being neutral in the face of authority had to do with my father. My dad was pretty authoritarian when I was a small boy. But I must immediately add that during the second half of his life, with no more children to educate, his attitude towards me, from adult to adult, was always kind and very cordial.

My brother and sisters, however, reminded me of childhood memories where I myself did not accept this authority; it often turned into a fight.

So, I kept this conditioning inside of me for many years.

Once I realized what was going on, I very quickly started to stay neutral towards authority. Today, my state of mind has changed. I am now able to say to myself, "They have their part to play and I have mine". *"No bad feelings, just business as usual"*.

When dreams come true

It is important to listen to your dreams because they give us direction in life. I am not talking of dreams that reside in our sleep but of those that doze in us and that appear in front of a good open fire or in a reclining chair, in the sun in our garden, or even during a walk in the fields or woods.

I remember when I was young, I dreamed that one day I would live in another country. My wish has been granted a thousand times! I have had the opportunity to become a citizen of the world through my work and my travels.

Personally, I remember that all the big decisions in my life that I made were when I was on vacation. These are the times outside the daily routine.

In 2014, I had the opportunity to attend a seminar in Morocco organized by Pierre S. of Es Sense inc.

The goal of the seminar was to have a 5-year life plan. At the end of the seminar, we all had to draw a picture of where we saw ourselves in 2019. We could draw our wildest dreams. My drawing included a professional component, a holiday component, a family component, a private life component, an international education component and a financial component. Our group met again in September 2019. As far as I'm concerned, all my dreams did come true.

So, there is no age to draw your dreams on paper and make them come true. However, the path between dreams and reality is called: "work, courage, perseverance and humility". The route is comparable to a mountain road that climbs to the top. It is rocky and winding but what an ecstasy when you get to the top!

The importance of a mentor

In Greek mythology, Mentor is the tutor of Telemachus and the friend of Odysseus. By assimilation, a mentor is an experienced, caring and wise counsellor who is fully trusted. We must not confuse "mentoring" with "coaching" which are two different concepts. (Wikipédia)

I speak on this topic because I really regret that I did not have the help of a mentor during my years abroad and my years as a CEO.

At 30-35 I was young and fiery. I had no experience in management, nor experience in running a profit centre. Within the Honeywell-Bull group I also had a lot of much older executives around me who didn't understand why a young guy like me could have such a great job. Years later, when I was running AMP with its 1,200 employees, I really missed the support of a mentor. My life would have been much more comfortable if I'd received such support.

Currently, it is me who performs this role discreetly for people much younger than me.

What are the essential elements that you should find in a mentor:

* He must be mature;
* He is often, but not necessarily, older than you;
* He must exercise or have exercised your current profession;
* He must have succeeded in this profession;
* Above all, he must have learned from his failures;
* He must be benevolent without feeling a sense of jealousy or frustration;
* He must be willing to give you the advice he wished he had received when he was your age.

Unlike a coach, a mentor gives you advice. He tells you what to do and what not to do. It is important that you each feel a bond and mutual respect for each other.

The first mentors in your life should actually be your parents. Unfortunately, it often happens that, in a family sphere, we carry beliefs and unspoken issues from previous generations that block instead of support you.

The first task of your mentor is to increase your self-confidence; his second task is to guide you through the pitfalls that run through your professional life.

Force yourself to find the right mentor for you. I assure you that if you look for it, you will find it. As far as I'm concerned, now that I'm a consultant, it's important to be able to share with others.

I know the importance of receiving support and skills in order to grow. I know it all the better as I have missed out on it at times in my life.

Accidents of life

The accidents of life also forced me to question myself. I believe that for many years I was a good husband to my wife and a good father to my children. However, when the time came for my children to leave home for their studies, (my daughter in Brussels and my son in Japan), I felt a huge void. For years, there had always been a lot of movement at home with the comings and goings of my children's friends.

After a few years of this feeling of emptiness, my wife and I decided to get separated. This choice was very difficult for me, considering all the consequences it entailed. I seeked help at the time from a Jungian psychologist (Carl Gustav Jung). She allowed me to find meaning, to listen to my intuitions, to relate to what was less rational in me. So, I started real personal development in my early fifties.

Through this development, I've noticed that my attitude has also changed at work. Colleagues have pointed out to me that I have become less intransigent and more attentive.

Each of us has or will have an accident in their life. For you, this will be a great opportunity to seek help, an invitation to question yourself.

My seminars in Germany

In 2009, I started a large training program for my sales network in several countries. The consultant responsible for the program, Daniela S., was German and spoke fluent French and Dutch. It was through her that I came into contact in 2010 with the institution "Institut für psycho-energetische Integration" in Germany. For 10 years now, once or twice a year, I have attended seminars on subjects that help us to better understand our human nature and therefore to better understand the nature of others. The seminar that has raised my awareness the most and that I have attended three times is on "Projection".

Projection

Explained succinctly, our view of others is filtered by our own experience. We can only see in others what is already present in us. If we admire someone for their talent, it's because somewhere, a well-hidden part of us also has this talent or at least was confronted with it in our early youth. Otherwise, we wouldn't be able to see it. If someone annoys us, it is because that person is awakening something hidden in us that we do not want to recognize. A practical application of this seminar found its way into my job interviews. I will talk about this in a later chapter.

Soul families

To some of you, this passage will strike you as totally esoteric. If so, go to the next topic.

When I attended my seminar in Morocco with 8 other CEOs, we were told about the Soul Families model, created by the Canadian Diane LeBlanc. There are four Soul Families: the **Builders**, the **Structuring Visionaries**, the **Peacemakers** and the **Facilitators**.

Each of us had to identify with one of these four Families.

My family is that of the Structuring Visionaries. When I am in the field of vision and structure, it gives me energy: it replenishes me and helps me flourish.

Each profession can be linked to a Soul Family.

Builders	Structuring visionaries
Entrepreneurs, start-ups, independent, business owners.	Members of the management committee in large groups; strategic consultants.
Peacemakers	Facilitators
HRDs, members of an NGO, etc.	Artists, painters, writers, photographers, filmmakers.

My priorities in life

Life is like a boomerang, everything that we project with intensity, both good and bad, always ends up coming back to us even stronger.

— *Paulo Amaro*

If I want to be successful in life, it is important that I am aligned with myself and in my pursuit of happiness.

Tony Hsieh, the boss of the Amazon subsidiary Zappos, set up a work culture a few years ago that was supposed to boost employee creativity by breaking down the traditional hierarchy and giving the company a human face.

He put forward three components: fun, passion and a meaningful life.

So, if you want a fun, passionate and a meaningful life, you need to make choices.

Question :

How would you prioritize the following subjects?

  * Health   * Family   * Hobbies   * Work

Personally, I put health first because you can forget about everything else if you are not healthy. This is why I have been doing step dancing once or twice a week for over 20 years.

My second priority in life is my family. Ever since my children and grandchildren came into the world, I feel like they are a part of me and through them I may leave a mark on this earth. I also feel that I have the responsibility to do everything I can in order to contribute to their happiness, leaving them complete freedom in their life choices. Then, my work and my hobbies would be equal because I must admit that, with rare exceptions, I have always had fun at work and on the trips that go with it. In these beautiful adventures, I also had the chance to meet and befriend extraordinary people.

I'll give you a few minutes to think about your priorities. After that, you will have to be honest with yourself. This means that when you have a choice to make in your schedule, priority 2 will take precedence over 3, no matter what!

Stress management

As CEO, you shouldn't fool yourself, your job will be stressful. Not only do you have a business to run with your teams, but you have a Board of Directors and shareholders to manage too.

Stress expresses your body's adaptation to a situation of external aggression. Your heart rate quickens, your blood and muscle pressure increase, and your adrenaline levels rise.

When stress is linked to a challenge to overcome, it becomes a powerful stimulus.

I remember well moments before decisive client meetings, before handing over a tender, before being interviewed by journalists from the financial press, during meetings with the unions, during board meetings where I had to defend my budget for the following year. During all these moments, I succeeded in harnessing my stress positively. Without it, I probably would have given a poorer performance.

Everything is therefore a question of balance. Too much stress could have damaged my physical and moral health. But since the stressful situations I experienced were manageable, stress became a real asset.

For the record, I must admit that my once or twice-weekly step dance classes did me a lot of good and helped me let off steam and let go of the excess tension accumulated during the day.

Vulnerability

Over the years, I have had less and less difficulty showing my vulnerabilities and admitting that I was wrong or that I had made a mistake. I believe that this had a positive effect on the way my employees regarded me. I became more human and approachable.

On the other hand, I'm not sure it was always smart of me to show this same vulnerability to my Board of Directors or shareholders. In fact, the higher up you are, the more scrutiny increases: excellence is expected of you 365 days a year. You can have one board where it goes badly, but you had better do well on the next. At Fountain, I knew 54 Boards of Directors. The last two went badly. You can guess what happened next...

Request for help

Asking someone for help is not always easy. For my part, I do not remember ever having been refused when asking for help. However, be aware of one point. Don't embarrass someone by asking them for something that will be difficult for them to give you.

I'll take the example of someone who is in between two jobs. Over the course of a career, there's a good chance this will happen to you too.

If you call someone to meet with him and ask him for information about his industry, he will be happy to receive you and at the end of the discussion, if you ask him to introduce you to one or two of his contacts, he will be happy to do so. One thing leads to another, you will have met dozens of people in a few weeks and it may be that one of them is looking for a profile like yours.

On the other hand, if you ask him if he has a job for you at his company, you embarrass him and you will leave the meeting empty handed.

So do not hesitate to ask for help around you. In 90% of cases, you will get a positive response.

The height of the CEO

Don't laugh if I tell you that my 1m 92 (6'4") has had some influence in my life.

Throughout my childhood and adolescence, I always found myself at the bottom of the row or behind in class because I was the tallest. So, I saw that as a disadvantage.

Strangely enough, when I was apprenticed as an army officer, I was placed on the left front of the parade and I was the only one who didn't have to turn my head to greet the colonel. It was then that I realized that being tall can also have advantages, no matter how small.

Very serious surveys have been made on the height of CEOs in the Fortune 500. They have found that 90% of CEOs are above average. They averaged 1m 83 (6'), about 6.4 cm (2.5") taller than the average American man. About 30% were 1m 88 (6'2") or more, which is only 4% of the total US population.

Other surveys have found that just 3% of CEOs are under 1m 70 (5'7") tall.

Fortunately, there are many exceptions to this rule. ☺

CHAPTER 4
My relationships in four universes

As CEO, we are fortunate to come into contact with a lot of people, both inside and outside the company we manage. By necessity, we have a public image.

This is the reason why I found it important to explore in this chapter the type of relationships linked to the different environments I hang out with: the business world, the networking world, the world of education and the world of partnerships.

The corporate world

— My relationship with my shareholders and my Board of Directors

In the trade press, we often talk about the CEO as if he was the one who decides everything and is equally responsible for the success and failure of a company. All public companies and most private companies also have a Board of Directors.

The Board of Directors is a body that represents the shareholders of a company. Its main role is to determine the strategic choices of the company and to control the actions carried out by the CEO and the management team. It is made up of directors and a chairman. In the boards of directors that I have known, some of the directors were themselves shareholders and others were independent.

As I wrote earlier, this CEO-Board relationship has not always been easy. Indeed, the objectives of some of my shareholders were to have a short-term return on their invested capital. For years, Fountain's dividend was approximately 20% on EBITDA and approximately 5% on the share price. On the other hand, I have also known brilliant and caring directors. They asked the right questions and were relevant in their suggestions.

Boards of directors have always been a welcome check on me. They have been a safeguard preventing my ego from taking up too much space as well as a fountain of ideas and an inexhaustible source of motivation.

So, I urge you if you are CEO to make sure you have a Board of Directors by your side or at least an advisory board if you are a 100% shareholder yourself.

— The importance of aligning with your shareholders

I cannot emphasize enough; it's important as a CEO to be aligned with the interests and values of your shareholders.

When you are appointed CEO, your shareholders ask you to raise the bar, to generate long-term growth, to increase annual EBITDA. For years these expectations were clear to me and having contact every two months with my shareholders suited me very well. Until the day when ...

In 2019, I followed a mentoring session with my friend Etienne VDK. He asked me if I was aligned with the true intentions of my shareholders and their fear of risk. At that time, my shareholders were a private equity group.

After some thought, I realized that at each bimonthly meeting, we talked about the results and the progress of the company without really having a frank conversation on the question of knowing: "What about you? How do you feel? "

So, it was very late in my professional life that I realized that a key element of success is alignment with your shareholders. Alignment is something of a much deeper nature than agreement on a project and its goals.

— What does it mean to be aligned?

Alignment is a set of priorities that represent my statements, my course of action, my behavior and finally my actions.

Personally, I always said what I was going to do and did what I said. So, I was aligned with myself and that has always conditioned my positioning within my professional environment.

On the other hand, I didn't ask myself enough whether I was aligned with my shareholders. Was I fully aware of what was going on in their heads or what they were discussing among themselves?

The only way to be aligned is to have regular conversations with each of them and always start the conversation with, "How are you feeling today?"

— How to deal with differences of opinion?

Peace is not the absence of conflict; it is the ability to manage conflict by peaceful means.

Ronald Reagan

It has happened more than once that I did not agree with my management or my shareholders. And you, has this also happened to you? Elementary my dear Watson!

So, the question is not so much whether we agree or not. The question is above all how to best manage a difference of opinion.

Here are four solutions. I leave you the free will of your choice.

* The first solution is when we keep quiet, we don't say anything, but we think no less. I have often experienced this with my own collaborators. The advantage that some of them have had with this situation is to keep their managerial position for over 30 years!

* The second solution is not to shut up, but to postpone your answer until later. A Swiss multinational CEO once told me how he managed his president and owner of the group. When his president suggested he do something he did not like, he simply replied: "I will think about it". As for me, it's not my style to postpone my answer. In terms of values, it could make me look like a coward. On the other hand, if the chairman was too emotional at the time of the discussion, it might indeed be smart to come up with an excuse and delay my reply.

* The third solution is to leave the company. It's a matter of conscience. This is a decision not to be taken lightly but can arise when all other options have failed to revert to a shareholder-CEO alignment.

* The fourth solution is to manage differences of opinion without going into open conflict.

Conflicts usually arise when people disagree on something that affects their own best interests or activates. Conflict is not an entirely negative thing. It's a part of our life and ultimately good things can come out of it. If a conflict exists with your shareholders, something is wrong with the state of affairs.

A common mistake I made was feeling sad and angry at the end of the day without being able to deal with it.

What helped me over time was trying to put myself in their shoes, asking them how they felt about it, what mattered most to them.

If you experience rage at such times, have the courage to calm down. Otherwise, your body language will betray you and you will lose all credibility.

Instead, just say how you feel. It will make your message more authentic. But remember to accompany your message with the appropriate reasoning. Having defused the emotional atmosphere around the table, your audience will listen and respond more rationally.

Properly managed conflict always results in more clarity and respect among participants. Problems or embarrassment that you or they were not aware of before will become palpable, and therefore, solutions will be found with confidence.

— Respect for oneself and others

In business life, each party has its own objectives: the shareholders (at least those who are not themselves the managers of their company), the employees and the CEO. The important thing is that the objectives of each party are respected by the other stakeholders.

The goal of the shareholder

The shareholder has put his money in a business that he does not manage himself. His interest is obviously the creation of value in the medium and long term while limiting its risk. To do this, he sets up a Board of Directors which will be responsible for defining the strategy as well as monitoring the good management of the company through an audit system. I assume that explained this way, other stakeholders will respect this goal.

The goal of the company's employees

Executives, employees and workers join a company to perform a job in which they can develop and evolve goals and objectives. When they signed their employment contract, they made a commitment to donate their time, intelligence and energy. In return, they receive a salary, paid vacation and a parachute in the event of dismissal. What are the needs of employees? They want to receive clear objectives, a high-performance work tool, a pleasant working environment, friendly colleagues, and above all, the feeling of being valued and respected by their superiors.

I once heard someone tell me that a company's assets left at 5 p.m. The personnel of your company are therefore its main asset. I assume that explained this way, other stakeholders could respect this goal.

The CEO's goal

Finally, there is you, the CEO. Your goal is to meet the challenge given to you by the Board of Directors. Build and develop your business with growth in turnover and profits. This role is both very rewarding and at the same time very thankless. In fact, you depend on the shareholder's agreement to inject more capital or to increase your level of indebtedness and you depend on your employees for the successful implementation in the field of the strategy you have developed and the objectives that you have made. In their book "Strategy Beyond the Hockey Stick", Chris Bradley, Martin Hirt & Sven Smit wrote the following: "What the CEO has under control are the big impulses of the company and these only represent 45% of the performance of their company".

Having run 7 companies, I can assure you that it is the CEO who makes the difference. Although he does not have a free hand for everything, he has the ability to surround himself well, to motivate well, to organize well and to communicate well. He is the one who has the most levers in hand to make a business successful or not.

I guess put it this way, other stakeholders should respect their CEOs.

The networking world

Tell me who you hang out with, I'll tell you who you are.

French proverb – unknown origin

One of the keys to becoming a CEO and being successful as CEO is having a high-quality network and being able to use it wisely.

— How to build your network?

I returned to Belgium at 40 in the mid-90s after having spent almost 15 years abroad. You might as well say that I had no network when I arrived. A few years later, I could call anyone in Belgium on the phone and have an appointment. How did I do it? I used the "snail" or "spiral" method.

When I started as CEO of PCB (Pharma Belgium), I immediately signed-up to become an active member of the ANGR (National Association of Wholesalers-Distributors of Specialty Pharmaceuticals). This association was part of a more global structure, FEDIS, currently Comeos, the organization which represents the entire distribution sector in Belgium. As I had 3,000 pharmacist customers, I also contacted the president of the APB, the national pharmacist's federation.

As I distributed medication to 30% of the pharmacists in Belgium, I organized a lunch-conference inviting all the CEOs of pharmaceutical companies based in Belgium to listen to my president, who came especially from France to be the guest speaker. Over 90% of CEOs answered the call, happy to have the opportunity to meet their colleagues and competitors.

With my direct professional network alone, I had succeeded in less than a year in making myself known to all the leaders in Belgium linked to the pharmaceutical and distribution sectors.

At the same time, I was sponsored to become a member of the Cercle Royal Gaulois and the Cercle de Lorraine. These are clubs that bring together a certain elite of Belgian society. My goal in becoming a member was not to do business but to meet my peers and people from other horizons.

Spending a pleasant evening with interesting and engaging people opens up new horizons to you. Unintentionally and without any ulterior motives, I realized years later that I personally knew CEOs who were active in sectors other than mine, but above all that I could call on if I needed information or specific help. Years later, I co-started the Cercle du Lac in Louvain-la-Neuve with 29 other co-operators. Its main mission was to promote networking and develop entrepreneurial spirit.

Then there were all the events organized by what is now called the Big 4: Deloitte, EY, KPMG and PwC. Through my presence at these events, I discovered more people from the Belgian business world.

What I did from scratch, each of you can do at your own level. I really encourage you to follow my "snail" or "spiral" method. First, look within your industry or profession to see what associations exist and become a member. Begin by refuelling in your industry and / or in anything related to your business.

At the same time, join one of the service clubs such as the Kiwanis, the Lions Club, the Rotary or the Round Table. On the one hand, you will be of service to the community by actively participating in the works they support, and on the other hand, you will expand your network of friends and businesses.

Then, don't hesitate to ask to be invited to major events organized by the Big 4 or other organizations.

I didn't mention the use of social media like LinkedIn. For me, these are great tools for maintaining an existing network, but not for building one. Indeed, I really believe in face-to-face social contact. The COVID-19 pandemic has obviously not been very favourable from this point of view. My advice is to encourage you to make and reconnect in the form of physical encounters (no joke intended, please ☺).

— A network has to be kept alive

The art of getting to know each other is one thing, but the biggest challenge is maintaining your network. I must admit that having managed several companies operating in very different sectors and each time headquartered in another country did not make it easy for me. Belgium is a country where there are two networks: one for Dutch speakers and another for French speakers. Very rare are those who are part of both, which is my case.

Reaching out

We all love to help, it's in our genes. Back in the days when GPS didn't exist, you could ask anyone for directions when you were lost on the road. The same is true in your professional life. Don't hesitate to ask, your wishes will often be granted.

Expressing thanks

You might be surprised, but a lot of people forget to thank the people who have helped them in their lives. In business, actions count more than anything. Thanking someone has to be our most important professional response. Forget about it and not only will you lose your network, but you will also put in jeopardy the people who put you in contact. So say thank you, again and again. It's free and it's such a pleasure.

Giving feedback

Do you remember when you did someone a favour or introduced them to someone you know? Didn't you want to know what happened next? The answer is obviously "yes!" Likewise, if someone is doing you a favour or introduces you to someone in order to find a new job, the least you could do is keep them up to date with what happens next. Even if the deal finishes six months later, do tell everyone who helped you find your new job. Nothing is more annoying for someone to have spent an hour or two with someone looking for a job and then to learn a few weeks or months later from the press, that he has been appointed CEO for this or that company. I have been through this myself and can tell you that the next time this person asks me for a favour, I will be absent.

The world of education

— The 7 lives of a cat - or how I once became a teacher

The announcement

It was in 2005. I asked Jean-Pierre B. professor at Solvay Brussels School of Economics & Management to prepare a Master class for some of my executives at Fountain.

During the preparation of this class, Jean-Pierre and I got to know and appreciate each other. One day, Jean-Pierre asked me: "You Pascal, who have lived and worked in three continents, would you like to teach in an MBA program at our university in Vietnam? The course would be "Intercultural Relations & Negotiation".

I told him that I had never given any classes in my life. He then replied: "Well, Pascal, it's not that difficult". I accepted his proposal and embarked on a new adventure... For 6 months, I researched and prepared a syllabus and with a Powerpoint presentation.

Summer arrived and I flew to Vietnam. My first hours in Saigon were quite emotional. I had opened a branch in this country 15 years before. Everything had changed so much ...

The classes

After a 17 hour flight, I arrived in Saigon. Then the classes started, 3 hours a day for 6 days with a group of students, all managers and already quite senior in their respective companies. I remember barely stepping outside all week, being so busy polishing my course and all the exercises.

However, rarely in my life had I experienced this feeling of excitement during and after each class. I had wonderful men and women in front of me. There was a fantastic interaction between us. I learned a lot from them about their ways and customs. Everything had changed so much in 15 years. For my part, I was put in a situation where I had to share knowledge outside of a professional context. In a company, it is the hierarchy that evaluates executives. Here, I was also going to be evaluated by my students. Finally, I learned that at the end of their year, they voted me "best teacher". What a proud moment!

Since then, I have returned to Vietnam every year except 2020 due to COVID-19.

When life offers you challenges, don't hesitate to accept them with open arms. Get out of your comfort zone. You will receive in return much more than what you have given.

— Transmission goes both ways

What I realized was that over the years I received, learned and grew. At 50, life gave me the opportunity to give back and share my knowledge and experience to others.

I realized that I could complement the theoretical course that I had prepared with my personal experiences in the USA, Europe and Asia. The students, all managers, could thus communicate with a CEO and discuss many subjects related to the daily concerns encountered in their home companies.

Personally, these annual trips over the past 14 years have allowed me to follow, year after year, the fantastic development of Asia, and Vietnam in particular. What a lesson for us Europeans, to whom everything is due, to see that there, families are bleeding dry to pay for the best studies for their children. It's exciting to see them so motivated to work tirelessly in order for their children to have a better life than them. It's so startling that in many ways Vietnam is ahead of us. For example, in the use of new technologies. What a joy, during my stays there, to give lectures to Solvay alumni, most of whom have been so successful in life. What a pleasure to share with them our common experiences as CEOs, to realize how things there are so different and, at the same time, so similar to ours. What a privilege to see Vietnam from the inside and to have made so many good friends there.

The partnership world

— How did I become a consultant?

There are people in your life who have the talent to take you out of your comfort zone. In my case, this person is called Jean-Pierre B. In September 2019, during our quarterly dinner, Jean-Pierre said to me: "Pascal, do you plan to stay CEO for a long time? Aren't you tired of having to report to shareholders? Why don't you become a consultant? You will take your life back into your own hands". His advice came at the right time because I was handing my job over to a young executive who would resume my role as CEO in January 2020. Being a change agent, I had just rewritten my objectives for the next five years with the following mission: to inspire and motivate people, help them to see that anything is possible and to empower them to act.

Life is well done, on 1 January 2020 I began my first project as a consultant for a beautiful private company in the textile industry. A few months later, in July, I met somebody who asked me to join his partnership.

— What are the big differences between the job of CEO and that of consultant?

The first difference is that the boss is my client and not me. He decides on the meeting dates; it is he who decides about the speed of change; and he sets the priorities. The first quality of any ex-CEO is having the necessary humility to recognize that he is no longer in charge and that he is there to help at the pace of the customer, not at his own. The second necessary quality is to always ask the question: how can I help? How can I inspire? What expertise can I bring to my client? My naturally structured way of working helps me a lot in this new profession.

— What does my new experience as an associate bring me?

The first impression I had when I joined a partnership was the sense of not feeling alone. We have formal meetings and also some short daily exchanges. What a pleasure to meet with peers, to understand each other at a glance, to be complementary, in other words, to all be aligned.

The second impression I had is not having to sell myself but rather to offer a service which, according to the needs of the client, can be carried out by one or the other consultant according to his own expertise.

The third impression I had was to feel responsible to my colleagues. If I make a commitment to call one of my contacts, I will keep that commitment. It gives us all a boost in our daily work.

And for me? A new chapter is opening in my professional life.

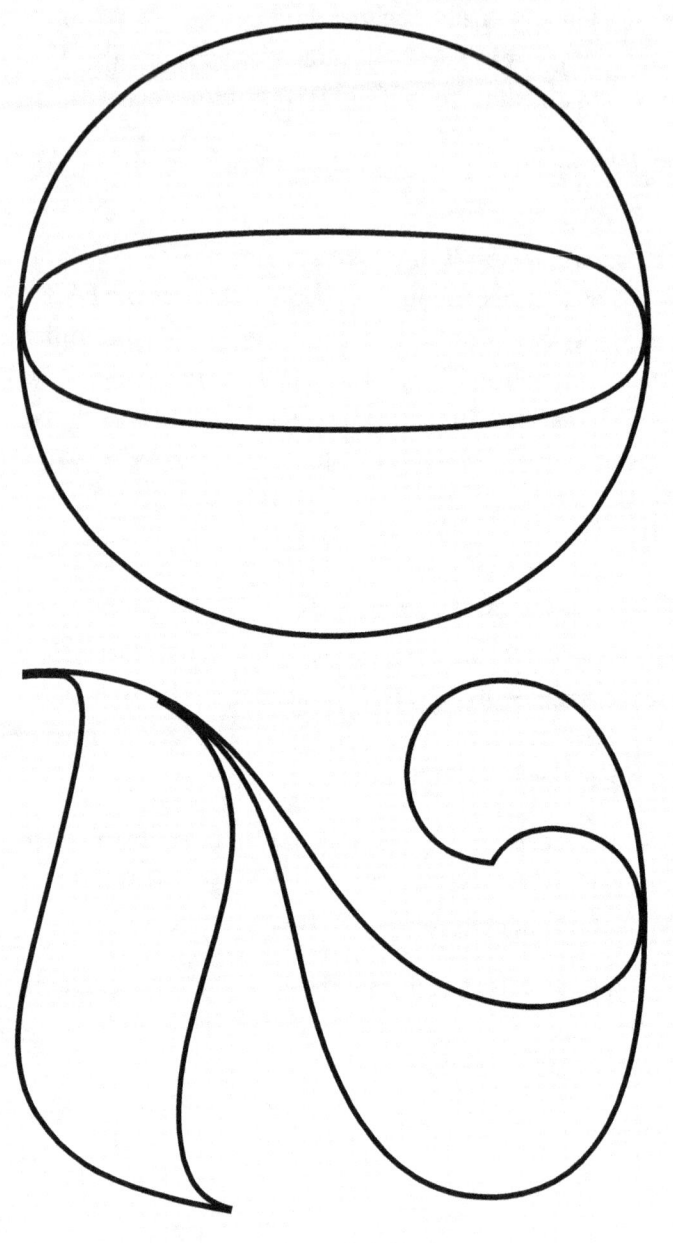

THEME 02

THE COMPANY'S LIFE

A company is above all a human family.
Of course, everyone has a role to play,
with their specific skills and functions,
but it is above all a story of alignment.
Working together to achieve the same goal,
a common vision, and values. A company
is also a place where you learn to delegate,
to trust, and to open up to others. Indeed,
customers, suppliers, shareholders and
bankers, all these external stakeholders will
be supporting pillars.

CHAPTER 1
Alignment with my teams

How to choose the right new employees?

What matters most to me when I hire an employee is their attitude. In a few seconds, I already have an idea through their gestures that I note in a box on the top right on a sheet of paper. Attitude is fundamental because every minute, every hour, every day that I spend with that person, it's their attitude that will make the difference.

In addition, each person involved represents the company and its values. Therefore, I have always asked my HR Director to meet an N-2 with the sole objective, not to check their skills, but to feel if, in his opinion, they correspond to the image I want to give of my company.

It is obvious that when hiring an employee, we look above all for their skills i.e., knowledge and know-how. As far as knowledge is concerned, it is easy: diplomas, languages, specialties. More difficult is to find out what is the real know-how of the person. Therefore, I like to ask them for some clear and personal examples with concrete situations. I take care that the person in front of me says "I" and not "we" and I look them in the eye to see if they are telling the truth and / or if they are comfortable.

We might not realize it, but we all make projections. In other words, we see in others what we carry inside us. I have already mentioned this in Chapter 3.

I personally cannot imagine cheating on my curriculum vitae. When hiring, following the principle of projection, I will believe everything that is written in a CV. I will not have the reflex to be suspicious about the veracity of the candidate's knowledge. However, in 2020, in the USA, 36% of candidates admit having lied on their CV. In France, 22% of CVs studied contained a serious lie.

One way to minimize this risk is to have a candidate meet with at least three people, with very different personalities and lifestyles. For example, one interviewer could be very analytical and rational; the other could be quite empathic; the third preferably a little borderline, someone who is not too used to following the rules. It is important that interviews take place individually so that interviewers do not influence each other. Then, everyone meets and shares the noticeable observations as well as the subtleties. My "borderline" colleague will probably notice if something is wrong with the candidate's speech. The candidate will only be hired if all three people are 100% positive.

How do you take your place when you arrive as a new CEO in an existing management team?

During my career, I joined 7 companies as an external CEO with unknown teams. I have to admit that I didn't always have the right attitude because I was too preoccupied with myself, and the desire to look good. Over time, I learned how to better manage myself. The first thing that matters as a newcomer is to put yourself in the other person's shoes. They are uncomfortable and are wondering what will happen to them.

The second most important thing is to get to know each of your new colleagues well: their family situation, their professional experiences, what they are proud of, their fears, etc. People like to talk about themselves and are happy that we spend time with them.

In addition to direct reports, in the first weeks it is important to get to know as many managers and employees as possible when the size of the company allows it. It's amazing what effect it has afterwards when you walk around the factory and people call you by your first name; the first meeting really breaks the ice.

The third thing, which is also very important, is to respect yourself. If the Board of Directors appointed me as CEO, it's because "I'm worth it". And so, even if it involves a significant change in the professional and private life of my future team, it is important that I respect myself. What does that mean ? It is important to know myself well and to pass on my values to others. Obviously, they will ask me what my goals are. It is obvious that at this point, having barely arrived, I cannot answer this question yet. So, I need the right modesty to say that it is too early and that it will take 100 days before I can answer their questions.

How do I encourage team members to accept each other?

— Learning to know each other

For a team to function well, it is essential that there is no suspicion among its members. What is special about human beings is that they are wary of anything they don't know. The role of a CEO is therefore to ensure that the members of their team get to know each other. The best way is to go offsite, do team exercises in a fun way and then have a good evening together around a table which could be followed by playing games. For the organization of a team event, I suggest that you call on specialized companies to ensure that each game has a specific psychological purpose.

For those who don't have the time or the budget for it, bowling followed by a dinner in a cozy restaurant will also do the trick.

During tough times, many bosses overlook these things. It's a mistake!

— Accepting each other

A management team is by definition made up of different profiles, such as a sales manager, an HRM, a plant manager, a financial manager and an IT manager.

Everyone will have built up a specific skill set throughout their career and have very different behaviors. This is why, on a permanent basis, the CEO must make sure that each member of his team accepts the other. A fairly simple way is for each member to invite one of their colleagues to "shadow" them for a day. What a great way to see what kind of skills your colleague uses in an area that you do not know yourself.

— Taking off the masks

Have you ever noticed that in the business world, executives and vice presidents have a tendency to emphasize their own importance? Because they have reached a certain hierarchical level, they believe that they must start to look down on lower level employees and even keep some distance from them. To be honest, and I have nothing against the French, but it was mostly in the Parisian offices that I noticed this.

Fortunately, with the arrival of the Millennium generation, all of that is changing. Having a certain status now is less important than working for something that makes sense and makes you feel fulfilled. So, I hope that in the future the dream of having a "corner window office" will be less important.

The role of the CEO is to say: "Take off your masks!" And it's up to them to set an example. Many CEO's currently sit amongst their teams and of course reserve room for confidential matters. Showing ourselves and others that we are human beings like everyone else but that each of us has a specific task to accomplish in the company is in itself a strong signal.

How do you make sure you have a well-diversified team?

A good management team is a team whose members have different characters, attitudes and energies.

— Character traits

Here below is a series of character traits. Play a game: choose the ones that suit you the most and those of your colleagues.

Extrovert or Introvert	Energetic or Passive
Methodical or Fuzzy	Confident or Distrustful
Sociable or Lonely	Original or Conformist
Conscientious or Distracted	Attentive or Dreamer
Idealist or Realist	Patient or Impatient

Fast or Slow	Enthusiastic or Indifferent
Idealist or Realist	Bold or Shy
Tolerant or Intolerant	Goofy or Prudent
Ambitious or Modest	Team player or Individualist
Rebel or Docile	Quiet or Thrilling
Authoritarian or Submissive	Impulsive or Thoughtful
Self-confident or Not sure of yourself	Curious or Blasé
Dynamic or Cool	Angry or Placid
SOURCE: REUSSIRMAVIE.NET	

This exercise clearly demonstrates the diversity and richness within each of us.

— The right attitude and the right behavior

Each culture and professional environment has its own codes. The way to address someone in Vietnam or in Japan is not the same as in the USA.

This same rule applies in the professional world. Every company has values and a culture that must be adhered to in order to create team spirit.

Here is a list of some attitudes and behaviors to adopt which are, in my eyes, universal.

Have a positive attitude	Enjoy teamwork
Have a strong work ethic	Be organized
Be reliable and efficient	Have a clear sense of priorities
Be involved	Be able to work under pressure
Communicate well	Be flexible
Be motivated	Be self-confident
Respect your colleagues	Know how to take a step back
Be relaxed and kind	Respect the rules

— The different energies in a company

A business is generally made up of three different components: commercial, industrial, and administrative & financial. Each of these components needs to work in a different energy.

The sales division has a red colored energy. It is the color of action, dynamism, emotion.

The production division has a blue colored energy. It is the color of responsibility, quality, and trust.

The support services such as finance, administration and IT have a green colored energy. It is the color of money, of stability. This color is calm and reassuring.

3 DIFFERENT ENERGIES

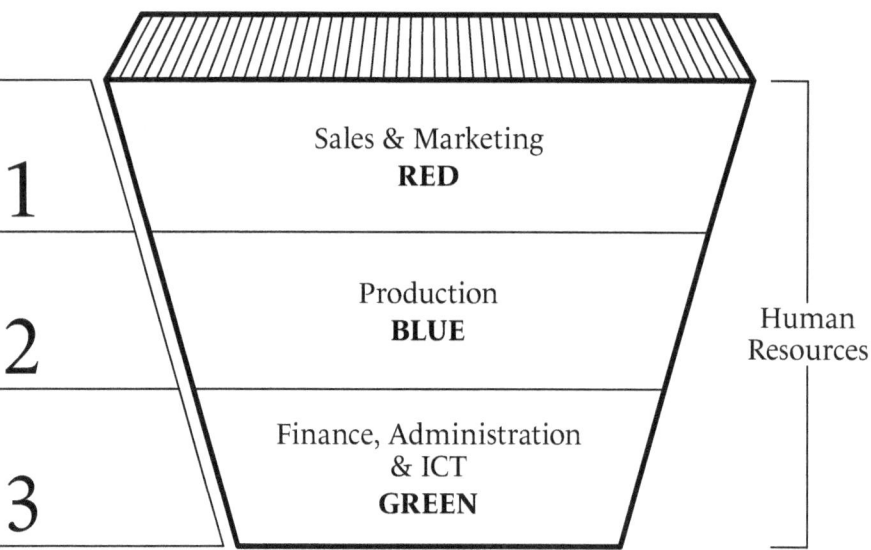

How to manage the tempo of a management meeting

How many of you remember endless meetings, where some topics were dragged out and others, for lack of time, were not even discussed?

— Be prepared

A good management committee requires good preparation i.e., an agenda that has been sent beforehand including agenda items, presenters and timing. During all the years that I have run companies, I myself sent the agenda to my colleagues. Most of the time at least 24 hours in advance and in some cases a little less depending on the circumstances. It was agreed that my staff would send me the topics that needed to be discussed ahead of time. As usual, it was always the people who sent me their agenda items late, and those who, during the management committee, raised a point that was not mentioned beforehand who jeopardized the timing of the meeting. Does that remind you of something?

— Keep it brief

Often, people go into too much detail that doesn't add to the meeting and distracts the participants. So, it's the CEO's role to play the policeman and ask the person to come to the point. I am often struck in meetings when two people who see each other regularly during the week discover new information from their colleague during the management meeting. Colleagues should discuss all relevant information prior to the committee meeting, to avoid controversies that take up time. When this happens I always interrupt and ask them to discuss this among themselves but not in the management meeting.

At the end of the meeting I always summarize the points that seemed most important. A Minutes of the meeting should be summed up in a series of bullets, not a 10-page document that no one will read.

— Respect allocated speaking time

In order to keep the meeting timing on track, it may be helpful to delegate the role of timekeeper to someone else beforehand. Haven't you noticed that it's always the same person who speaks the longest and the same person who says nothing? I see you are smiling as you read this but given the cumulative hourly cost of the salaries of the managers present, it is well worth paying attention to this as well.

How to embrace the values of the company

Many companies have already spent a day offsite with their senior executives and agreed to a list of values which was then transcribed into a document. Often, these values can be found alongside the company's mission and vision on their website.

Take the test. Ask any member of a company to list its values for you. Nine times out of ten, they will not know them or will only be able to list two or three. This is a shame because a company's mission or vision can change over time, depending on its evolution or mergers and acquisitions. On the other hand, the values of a company are unalterable. You have companies in Germany that have existed for 300 years and whose values are still the same.

— How to keep your company's values alive

Personally, I think you should not have more than five or six company values. It forces you to prioritise. I take an example of values chosen by a German company.

1. We focus on our customers every day

2. We are continuously improving

3. We respect and encourage each other

4. We act as entrepreneurs

5. We keep to our commitments

One of my associates, Jan DM, has developed a tool that allows the values of a company to be kept alive by all the employees in a simple way.

Each value results in 6 behaviors and each behavior in 6 practical tips. The employee has access to a software where they choose two behaviors that affects them and that they would like to work on. They receive a list of 12 tips by email. Their boss receives the same list. So, at each coaching meeting, they explain the actions they have taken following the advice they have received. Imagine the result and the punching power that this can give to 3,000 employees!

How to work in an effective way with men and women in a company

— Gender diversity

The cliché of an era when women were secretaries and men were bosses is long gone in modern society.

Throughout my career, I have had the opportunity to interact with both sexes, and over time, I began to better understand the differences between men and women in their attitudes and behavior. In writing this text I know that I am walking on quicksand and that inevitably, I will be borderline with a caricature. Still, I want to bring up the subject because I would lie if I said that there are no behavioral differences between the two sexes.

I will start by describing what I have experienced in the labor force in logistics. When I was CEO of PCB, a pharmaceutical distributor, we organized 10,000 deliveries a day to 3,000 pharmacies. All the staff who did the selecting in our logistics centers were women. The selection error rate was 0.2%. The answer I was given back then is that a woman is quite capable of concentrating on her task when her thoughts may be elsewhere. Commonly, it is said that a woman can easily do several things well at the same time.

A few years later, I was CEO of AMP, a press distributor. Every day we delivered to 6,000 shops. Since magazines and newspapers are heavy, our labor force was 100% male. Guess what the error rate was? Well, it was 5%. This speaks for itself, right?

In all repetitive jobs, in factories or offices, for the encoding of orders or invoices where error must be reduced to a minimum, women perform much better than men.

In terms of management, I also had the chance to work with women. What I have often perceived is their lack of self-confidence and their desire for perfection. When I was CEO of Fountain, a coffee machine supplier, Maud M. was the best sales manager in our company and was based in Paris. I remember her calling me once or twice a week to ask my opinion on something. Since her cases were so well prepared, the only thing I had to do was listen to her and say "yes". After 30 minutes of talk she was motivated again for a few days.

My most enjoyable time as CEO was when I ran a barbecue company in Kortrijk, a city near Bruges in Belgium. More than half of my board was made up of women. What a pleasure to work in such a professional atmosphere. Each subject that was presented to me had been prepared with so much care. My only concern was sometimes having to manage the susceptibilities between women, which for me was easy.

I have also had the opportunity to meet female CEOs. Once again, what impressed me and what I remember was their professionalism and attention to detail.

— And what about the ego in all of this

My biggest difficulty as CEO was having to manage the egos of some of my staff. This resulted in endless discussions about the number of accessories for their company car or the title on their business card; I also remember some snobbish attitudes towards me when I arrived as the new CEO in their company. It went something like this: *"I have been doing this job for 20 years, there is nothing you can teach me!"* Personally, I could handle these situations, but it became more awkward when, in one of my companies, one of my directors refused to communicate with a young female marketing manager. This young person then had to go through me so that I passed her request to her director. It's true, I assure you! As burlesque as it is, this story shows you how life in a company is not always as ideal as you would like it to be and that there is still some way to go when it comes to the gender issue.

I don't remember having to deal with a single ego issue with all the women I've worked with. This is to their credit. One great quality that I have noticed in them is their ability to always question themselves.

How to handle a serious crisis in the company

Each CEO will have to manage a serious crisis in their career. However, I do not wish anyone to go through the crisis I experienced.

— The crisis

It's a Monday morning in 2009. I'm working in my office. It's looking like a quiet week.

We are approaching the holiday season. The previous Friday we had just celebrated Christmas with the entire Brussels team of the Fountain group in a beautiful location surrounded by a snowy park.

It's 10 a.m. when the phone rings. It's the police. *"Hello Sir, are you Pascal Wuillaume, the CEO of Fountain? Yes, it's me. Do you know Mr. Michel M? Yes, he's my CFO. Well sir, I have the sad news to announce that Mr. M died this morning in a house fire with his two young children. His wife was with the physiotherapist at the time. She is currently in shock in hospital".*

Within seconds, 1000 things start spinning simultaneously in my head. Michel had worked with me at AMP and he joined me a few years later at Fountain. He had become a friend. I wanted to scream but my duty was to inform my staff as soon as possible of this tragic event. Filled with emotion, I also had to worry about the repercussions of this event on our company and in particular, on our stock market listing. Shit! Anything but not that ... and yet, I had to keep a close watch on things. I was after all the CEO of the company. The 2009 figures had to be ready in the coming weeks. There was no need to create a panic. The most important thing was to go to the hospital as quickly as possible to see Michel's wife Nancy.

I walked out of my office and quickly gathered the headquarters staff in the meeting room. The news of this tragic event brought screams and tears. Then I walked to the Belgian subsidiary and our small production unit. Same scenario, cries and tears. I tried despite the shock to keep a cool head. I then called the bosses of my subsidiaries and I, with my marketing team, put in place a crisis unit in charge of taking all calls from the non-financial press. I also asked to set up a small internal blog so that all the staff could access real time news.

I drove to the hospital. Nancy was in floods of tears and had taken tranquilizers. She had just lost her husband Michel and her baby Phaedra, who was two and a half years old. There was also Theophile, four years old, a child from a previous relationship. He was with them for the weekend.

A few days later, in front of a packed crematorium, I gave a eulogy about Michel with, next to me, a large and two small coffins. In front of me, mothers, sisters, family, staff from Fountain and AMP where Nancy worked, as well as a few board members.

Then very quickly I had to find a new CFO, reassure the financial press and take the reins in order to ensure maximum business continuity. In the evening, at home, I let my emotions run free and I cried all the tears in my body. Every time I relate this episode, I still have tears in my eyes. I accompanied Michel's wife in her various administrative formalities during the following months. I was amazed at her courage and ability to rebound.

Weeks later, my board members congratulated my handling of the crisis. They told me that I had reacted in a very courageous, very professional and very human way.

— What I remember from this crisis

Whatever happens in our life, we have to remember that we are above all human beings. So, there is no need to hide our feelings at such times. As CEO, however, our duty is above all to keep our head on our shoulders, to comfort the teams, to reassure the market and to put everything in place to ensure the continuity of the business. The task of the CEO is to ensure, whatever happens, the interest and sustainability of the company. This should be remembered even if this is a tough matter to accomplish.

How to help your teams to surpass themselves

If you want your business to be successful, you have to make sure your teams always aim higher, that they open up to new horizons, and that they keep their skills up to date.

One way to help executives aim higher is to expose them to examples outside their company. That's why I gave Jack Welch's "Winning" book to all of my senior executives.

Although the vision and methods of the former GE boss are no longer relevant to the current generation, they were great examples for me. I also offered a personalized MasterClass to ten executives from our company. The courses were spread over a period of six months and were organized at the time by the Solvay Business School.

This exercise allowed me to have people in my company who could instill new ideas and new ways of working to other staff members. Indeed, at the end of their MasterClass, they each presented a project for a concrete implementation in their environment.

How to work while delegating

You may have noticed in your professional life that some people around you easily delegate tasks to others and others have difficulty doing so. They are more in control. It is true that you will feel more competent than your collaborators in many areas and for things where you feel less, you will delegate easily so that you no longer have to worry about it. Well, you are wrong!

When I was a young executive in New York, I pinned on my wall a quote from Ronald Reagan about his management style. This is what he said:

* Surround yourself with the best
* Delegate
* Control

Many years later, I must thank Reagan for his message which I have retained and applied throughout the rest of my career.

— Surround yourself with the best

Every time I joined a company as a new CEO, there was already a management team in place. So, I did not have the opportunity to choose my direct collaborators.

Your job as CEO is to make sure that you are surrounded by the best team members for the tasks they have to accomplish. You have been appointed for a mission to succeed. So, the only way to do that is to make sure you have the best team around. It is thanks to your team that you will be successful.

Some of you might find my words quite harsh. But if you do not have the courage to change the composition of your close staff, knowing that they ar incompetent, how are you going to explain to your board members that this or that is not your fault but that it is one of your team members who is incompetent. Their answer will be simple: you are the CEO. So, it's up to you to solve your problem, otherwise it's you who will have the problem.

Having said that, I am not asking you to make a clean sweep as soon as you arrive: that would be a serious mistake. Give yourself time and ask yourself for each member of your close staff: is this person going to be a vector for the success of the company? If your answer is "yes", no worries. If your answer is "yes, but" ask yourself why. If this is a problem that can be solved by training or coaching, don't hesitate to suggest it. On the other hand, if it is a problem of inadequate attitude, if it is a problem of lack of benevolence, you have only one solution: Let them go.

— Delegate

Delegating is not an easy task. Delegating does not mean "laissez faire" and we will discuss that later. Delegating requires first to put on paper the main mission that you expect from your employee and then a breakdown in a set of tasks to be accomplished in a given time. Make sure your employee agrees with his tasks and everything that it requires. Give him time to return with a revised proposal. Once everything is clear between the two of you and your other staff members, schedule a short weekly meeting with each of your direct staff members.

— Control

This weekly meeting is mainly used to ensure you are aligned on a number of points. The topics I like to cover in our discussions are:

* Concrete points
* Management issues
* Competence issues
* Difficulties related to alignment

The first three topics are fairly straightforward to understand. The subject of alignment is more delicate because it is more complex and more intimate. Indeed, when we feel well aligned, it allows us to work well.

Aligned with their feelings

When I start a conversation, I ask the question: "How are you feeling?" If the answer is "I feel great!", we continue with other subjects. However, if they show feelings of sadness or frustration, it is important to investigate the matter further before tackling any other topic.

Aligned with other managers

It is also important to ask them the question: "How are you doing with your colleagues?" Don't worry. If something is wrong, they will tell you right away. People love to talk about their coworkers, especially about what is wrong. This will allow you to make up your own mind, locate the problem and possibly help the other person solve it. Indeed, for the success of the company, cohesion between the teams is essential.

How to understand the underlying reasons behind a difficult relationship

If you've ever had the opportunity of managing a team, have you ever noticed that with some of your people, the flow is good and with others, the relationship is difficult?

Personally, I was very young when I ran my first company, and I had a management team that was much older than me. So it wasn't that easy to command respect and bring my whole team together towards a common goal. There were always one or two people who were against change.

It wasn't until much later, reading Dweck's "Mindset" book, that I understood why some of my staff agreed with my ideas for change and others didn't.

Some had an open mindset and others a closed mindset. I simplify a little because the reality was obviously more nuanced.

Those with closed mindsets saw me as a threat. They thought they knew everything and that I had nothing to teach them. Being new, they saw me as a danger as I risked breaking the beautiful, comfortable cocoon they had built over the years and in which they felt comfortable. I was actually forcing them out of their comfort zone. That's why I had this weird feeling of not being understood in my change management process.

As I was CEO of Fountain for 9 years, I was able, over time and following natural departures, to hire younger, more enterprising executives with an open mindset. They knew they still had a lot to learn. They knew that if they made mistakes, we would talk about it; then we would correct them. They felt supported by me in their efforts and were therefore less afraid of taking risks. It was all beneficial to their business growth.

Surprisingly, I have found the same issues with open and closed mindsets in other companies that I have run since then.

Singularly, most of the people who stayed in touch with me in the years after I left their company were all open-minded, eager to move forward and learn. Most have to date already changed jobs once or twice with great promotions and excellent salary packages. Some have also become CEOs themselves.

CHAPTER 2
Leadership assessment tools

The three characteristics of a good leader

A few years ago, I gave a talk in Hanoi, Vietnam on the characteristics of a good leader. The COVID-19 crisis has underlined this need for leadership. The three characteristics of a good leader that I will describe to you are universal; they are valid in all countries and are unchanging over time. A good leader must be a visionary, a good communicator and a good organizer.

— Vision

A true leader has a vision. They must have a clear picture of the future and a clear vision of their business. Specifically, the direction it should take and the goal it should reach. So, think carefully about whether you have a clear picture of the future of your company and its goal.

— Communication

A vision without communication is useless. Look around you, all the great known visionaries of this world are good communicators. In the business world, names like Bill Gates, Steve Jobs, Jeff Bezos, Elon Musk, Larry Page, Mark Zuckerberg, Jack Ma all resonate in our heads and, one way or another, they had or will all have an influence on our way of life. If each of them had not been, in their own way, great communicators, their companies would never have enjoyed the success they are enjoying today.

By communicating with a force of conviction, they instilled extraordinary energy in their employees by leading them towards ambitious projects.

They also used their communication skills to promote their products and their company to the outside world. Many other visionaries have remained anonymous and their vision, however relevant, was useless. If you think you are having difficulty communicating in public, be trained. You are not always born a good communicator, but you can always learn to become one.

— The implementation or the "Make it happen"

What has often struck me in my life are fine speeches, full of good ideas, but that never amounted to anything. Many great political figures have carved key phrases in our collective memory. Unfortunately, few of them were able to turn their slogans into reality. The reason is mainly related to their lack of organization and their inability to achieve meaningful results. This also applies to the corporate world. A good vision well communicated but without concrete results is useless. Later in my book, I will talk about change and using certain tools to successfully implement those changes and see tangible results.

WHAT ARE THE KEY CHARACTERISTICS OF A LEADER ?

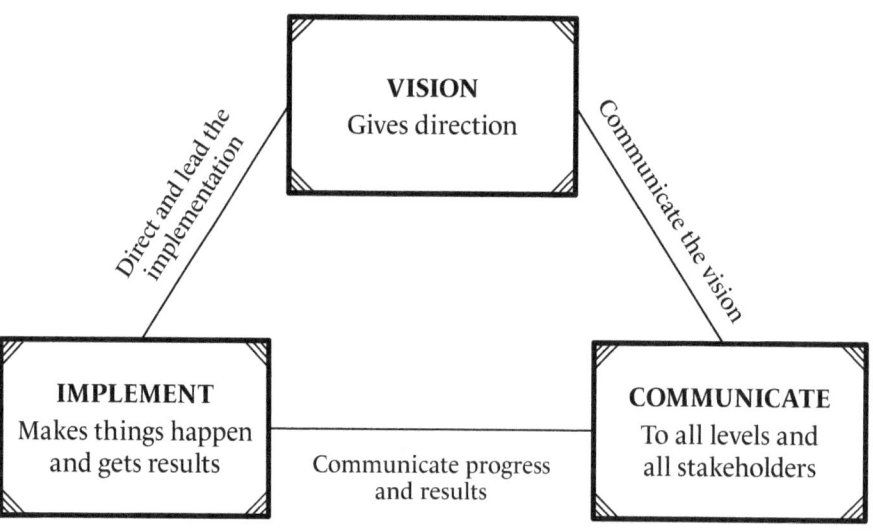

The differences between a leader and a manager

In the corporate world you will find a lot of good managers but few real leaders.

Below is a table of a list of behaviors that describe the differences between managerial qualities and leadership qualities. However, this table is not exclusive because a good leader must also have several qualities of a good manager, but not all! Guess which…

MANAGERS	LEADERS
Administer	Innovate
Maintain	Develop
Focus on systems/structure	Focus on people
Control	Trust
Think short-term	Think long-range
'How/when?'	'What/why?'
Focus on the bottom line	Focus on horizon
Imitate	Originate
Accept	Challenge
Are good soldiers	Are own people
Do things right	Do the right thing
Like order	Accept ambiguity
Create check lists	Create roadmaps

— How do you end up being a good leader?

A good leader is difficult to define but easy to recognize. Some are born leaders and others learn to become one. A good leader is not only about inspiring others: they must first of all get to know themselves well. You will find around you a multitude of leaders who each have their own unique personality and skills. The purpose of this chapter is not therefore to impose on you a unique model of leadership but, on the contrary, to help you get to know yourself well. So, you can use your character and skills as levers for your own success. You will get there by knowing your weaknesses and strengthening your strengths.

Indeed, no leader is perfect. Each person has personality traits with their strengths and weaknesses. But not everyone is aware of this. This is why a periodic check-up of your leadership skills is equivalent to a blood test at the doctor. The results indicate that you have too much of this and too little of that. And continuing the metaphor, you have to be careful to reduce the excesses and make up for the deficiencies.

Personality tests

There are several psychological assessment tools that determine the psychological type of a person. One of the best known and most intense is the Myers Briggs Type Indicator (MBTI®) developed in the 1960s by Isabel Briggs Myers and Katherine Briggs. Their questionnaire is built on psychological types developed by Carl Jung, but in a more accessible format for managers like us.

The Myers Briggs Type Indicator (MBTI®) test defines 16 different personalities.

The result for me is ENTJ: Extraversion (E), Intuition (N), Thinking (T), Judgment (J).

This very popular personality test is a good starting point for your leadership journey. It is important to know what type of personality you are. This test has 16 distinctive personality types built from four main psychological functions: sensing, intuition, thinking and feeling. You can have multiple personalities but only one will be dominant.

You will easily find many sites online that offer free tests. However, my suggestion is, if possible, to seek help from a certified coach. He will provide you with the appropriate feedback on your score depending on the context in which you are taking the test.

This is how I understood the MBTI® test.

Extraversion (E) or Introversion (I) – Orientation of your energy

The energy of *Extraverts (E)* comes from their interaction with people and things outside. They are quite active, expressive and sociable.

The energy of *Introverts (I)* comes from within themselves. While Introverts are more reserved, their actions will generally be more thoughtful. Here's a little tip that you will find useful in life: If you want to know what an Extravert is thinking, listen to him. If you want to know what an Introvert is thinking, ask him.

Sensing (S) or Intuition (N) – Information collection

Sensing people (S) are generally down to earth with a very practical side. They are attentive to the facts and realities of the world around them.

People with *Intuition (N)* on the other hand, are more imaginative and creative. They are more interested in the connections between things and the possibilities that can arise. They trust their instincts.

Thinking (T) or Feeling (F) – Decision making

Thinkers (T) evaluate facts and make judgments based on objective criteria. Their decisions are based on rules and principles and not on their values. They have a strong analytical mind and therefore are inherently logical.

Feelers (S) base their assessment on personal or interpersonal values. They are sensitive and empathetic; they seek harmony and are subjective in their reasoning

Judging (J) or Perceiving (P) – Action mode

People who are *Judging (J)* like to live in a structured, orderly and predictable environment. They are in control and like to make decisions. They are well organized and formal.

Perceivers (P) on the other hand love experiments. So, they don't have a problem with last minute plan changes. They are therefore flexible, curious and non-conformist.

My professional score is ENTJ. However, if I do the same test in another context during my vacation, it could be slightly different. We have a dominant personality but also many sub-personalities. Depending on the context, it is therefore possible for you to favor one of your sub-personalities over another.

I like the MBTI test because it is based on Carl Jung's studies and his invention of psychological types.

The bottom line for you is that each human being is specific with his strengths and weaknesses. Taking this test as a team will allow everyone to better discover the personality traits of their neighbor. If you manage to create a team with MBTI profiles adapted to the missions that are assigned to them, you will then have the best team in the world!

— The Myers-Briggs (MBTI®) table with 16 personality types

ISTJ Administrator	**ISFJ** Protector	**INFJ** Visionary	**INTJ** Perfectionist
ISTP Craftsman	**ISFP** Conciliator	**INFP** Idealist	**INTP** Thinker
ISTP Entrepreneur	**ESFP** Entertainer	**ENFP** Communicator	**ENTP** Innovator
ESTJ Organizer	**ESFJ** Nurturer	**ENFJ** Facilitator	**ENTJ** Leader

— The Platinum Rule®

The other personality test is called The Platinum Rule®, by Tony Alessandra. This test analyzes four behaviors found in society. It is easily found in English on the Internet.

The vertical axis depicts you as *"open"* and therefore people-oriented or *"guarded"* and therefore more task-oriented.

The horizontal axis depicts you as *"direct"* with a fast pace or *"indirect"* with slower and more thoughtful reactions.

Depending on where you find yourself on the graph, you will be more: *"director"*, *"socializer"*, *"relater"* or *"thinker"*.

OPEN
[People-oriented]

RELATERS

- ✓ Slower/relaxed, prioritise relationships
- ✓ Seek acceptance
- ✓ Listening, teamwork, follow-through
- ✓ … But oversensitive, slow to begin action, lack global perspective
- ✓ Fear sudden changes and instability
- ✓ Irritated by insensitivity and impatience
- ✓ Under stress may be: submissive, indecisive
- ✓ Security through friendship, cooperation
- ✓ Friendly, functional, personal workplace

SOCIALIZERS

- ✓ Fast/spontaneous, prioritise people
- ✓ Seek participation and applause
- ✓ Persuading, motivating, entertaining
- ✓ … But inattentive to detail, short attention span, low follow-through
- ✓ Fear loss of social recognition
- ✓ Irritated by routines, complexity
- ✓ Measures personal worth by acknowledgements, applause, compliments
- ✓ Interacting, busy, personal workplace

INDIRECT
[Slower-paced]

DIRECT
[Faster-paced]

THINKERS

- ✓ Slower/systematic, prioritise tasks
- ✓ Seek accuracy, precision
- ✓ Planning, systematising, orchestration
- ✓ … But perfectionist, critical, unresponsive
- ✓ Irritated by disorganisation, impropriety
- ✓ Security through preparation, thoroughness
- ✓ Measures personal worth by precision, accuracy, quality of results
- ✓ Formal, functional, structured workplace

DIRECTORS

- ✓ Fast/decisive, prioritise goals
- ✓ Seek productivity, control
- ✓ Administration, leadership, pioneering
- ✓ … But impatient, insensitive to others, Irritated by inefficiency, indecision
- ✓ Security through control, leadership
- ✓ Measures personal worth by impact or results, track record and process
- ✓ Efficient, busy, structured workplace

GUARDED
[Task-oriented]

CHAPTER 3
About sales

B2B business (business between two companies) success begins with the selling of products or services. This is why I find it necessary to review all the aspects of this business and the role that the CEO plays within it.

The right commercial profile

Having worked on three continents and in several sectors, I have noticed similarities in character traits between the different salespeople that I have had the opportunity to oversee.

— Curiosity

Curiosity is innate. Some children stay in their mothers' skirts and others systematically go off to discover new experiences. Some might even complain about their behavior. Personally, I find that curiosity is a great character trait that must be present in all salespeople. Indeed, this talent will help them to seek new opportunities, and once the contact is established, to find out through a dialogue with their interlocutor the product or service that their prospect really needs.

— Human contact

A salesperson must love interaction. They must be outgoing and human contact will give them the energy to be successful in their job. To fully understand and meet your customer's needs, listening should be a key feature. If you have an introvert in front of you, you'll be asking them the right questions. If the person is outgoing, you will just listen, and the right information will come to you effortlessly.

— Listening

For years, I thought that I was a good listener and that I understood my interlocutor well. I thought that I was an active listener. I was interested in what people had to say, I nodded and asked questions. However, many people told me: "*Pascal, you are not listening*". This annoyed me for years until one day, during a coaching session, Daniela S., my coach, told me: "*Pascal, when you interrupt a person who is speaking, the following is happening inside them. By interrupting the course of their reflection and thoughts, it abrogates their reasoning. They can't just pick it up where they left off and they have to start all over again. It also causes the release of cortisol, the stress hormone. They will therefore have a negative feeling towards you*". I never thought of that. I saw it from my point of view, i.e., understanding the message. I hadn't understood the other person's point of view, that is, to respect them in the continuity of their thoughts.

Since then, I always have a coin in my pocket that I squeeze tightly to force myself to react only after the other person has finished talking. After all these years, I must say that depending on who I speak to, it works between 50% and 80% of the time. It's a start...

— Energy

All salespeople must radiate a communicative energy. If they are an extrovert, this will come naturally and effortlessly. It is through their positive energy that they will persuade the client to sign, and not through their explanations. Indeed, the act of buying is a subjective choice that is primarily directed by our emotions. Admit it, few of you buy a car on the basis of purely rational criteria. Some will of course, but after having already chosen the brand and model.

The customer is always right

Every time I started a new CEO assignment in a company, I took care to meet my clients, large or small, pretty quickly, in order to gather information on several levels.

I would gather information about the client, their business and their expectations in general and especially towards us. So they were usually more open to talk to me. I was not there to sell but to listen. A customer is less guarded and is more inclined to answer questions without apprehension from a CEO than from a salesperson. This is why they will easily talk about their business, competition, immediate and long-term needs, and appreciation of our products or services. Often, they even go one step further and give me advice on how to beat my competitors.

I always assume that the customer is right. It is my company that must adapt to their needs and not the other way around. Sometimes my business doesn't have the right offering. It is then up to my internal teams to calculate the profitability. If their request is unreasonable or if my industrial tool requires large investments that will never be profitable, we will warn the client that, despite our efforts, we cannot respond positively to their request.

Many companies pay outside consultants to do market research on their industry. For my part, I suggest that you visit your customers and prospects more often. You will probably gather just as much information.

I must add to this that, when I met with customers, I was always accompanied by the sales representative in charge of the account. I never entered into a negotiation with a client unless it had been agreed in advance with the sales rep.

Selling

Selling is all about finding the right solution for your customer and making their life easy. If they are smiling, it means it will be beneficial. The role of the salesperson is to make his business resonate with that of his client. A bad salesperson is someone who says to his client, *"I agree with you, but my boss won't"*. By doing this, they put themselves forward and do not create resonance. On the contrary, they annoy the client and will risk losing him.

Cultural influence on the sales activity

Having had the opportunity to work in three continents, I have seen everything and its opposite. To keep things simple, I'll tell you about my experience in the USA and in France.

During my 5 years in the USA, I followed sales representatives on several occasions. This is when I really understood the expression "the customer is king". The role of the salesperson was really to find win-win solutions. Respect for the customer is deeply rooted in American culture.

It is always dangerous to get bogged down in clichés, but the worst examples I have known were in France. Many salespeople, especially in the Paris region, sold to have their bonus at the end of the month without worrying at all about whether the solution suited the customer or whether they were solvent. Rather, their modus operandi was to get rich off the customer's back. I remember a rather hilarious anecdote from my boss in Paris who did not agree to the terms of a major Spanish client. He then said to me: *"Pascal, we're going to have a tough negotiation and make them suffer"*.

Fortunately, with the recent growth of international online shopping sites, the standards of customer respect have hugely changed. I suggest to those who criticize sites like Amazon, first match their excellent level of customer service.

The CEO is the N°1 sales representative of his company

When you look at companies that far outperform their competitors, you often have a charismatic CEO at the top who knows how to be present when big negotiations take place. In 2008, NASA had to choose between SpaceX and Boeing to build a new spacecraft to send astronauts into space. They ultimately opted for SpaceX' offer over Boeing's. In this case, it was Elon Musk who really got his shirt wet to win this deal of the century. I doubt his competitor's CEO did the same.

Personally, and in much more modest circumstances, I remember having mobilized a whole multidisciplinary team in France to respond to a RFP from the OGF (a large French group operation in the funeral business). Every night at five o'clock for over ten days, I would set up a teleconference to answer all and any questions. I was also present in Paris with the sales representative in charge of the account in order to defend our case. We were fortunate to win this RFP. I learned incidentally afterwards that none of our competitors' high-level management had shown up in person.

Selling is the main reason for a successful business

The financial flow of a business can be compared to a funnel. The more cash that goes in from the top through sales, the more likely it is to come out at the bottom as profit. Many companies subcontract production, administration, logistics or transport. However, you never subcontract your sales network! After all, the customer must be the center of attention in any business. It also doesn't mean that all salespeople have to be employees. Medium-sized companies may have independent agents or distributors for their export sales. However, it is essential that they are managed by a central sales department. The commercial and marketing offer must be coherent, especially today when the whole world is connected. Your websites must therefore have the same images and messaging all over the world.

The different energies of the B2B sales cycle

You will find thousands of websites that explain how to go through the stages of the B2B sales cycle before signing a contract.

My goal here is rather to talk about the different energies that go into a sales cycle. If channeled well, your success will be assured.

Emotion plays a key role in buying and therefore also in selling. A human being is physical, mental and emotional. If our mind helps us memorize, plan and structure, it is with our emotions that we fulfil our desires.

The initial contact between the seller and the buyer will therefore be strongly linked to emotion. The emotions of the seller will try to please the buyer whose emotion seeks to fulfil the desires of his business by buying the right product at the right price. We are here in a red colored energy.

If this phase goes well, we can move on to the following phases, which are the analysis of the needs and the sales pitch. During these two phases, it is important for the salesperson to be assisted by a technical specialist. The latter will be able to counter possible objections thanks to their excellent knowledge of your product or service. We are here in a blue colored energy.

Then come the last two stages which are negotiation and conclusion. Here we are again in the emotion: the seller must reassure the buyer that he is making a good purchase at the right price. We are here again in red colored energy.

If some salespeople fail to close a deal, it is often because they don't have the right energy at the right time.

The hunter and the farmer

Every company should have at least two types of salespeople. The hunter and the farmer. The hunter sets out to conquer new customers. The farmer builds on the portfolio of existing customers either through additional sales or through new services.

Although both are salespeople, their profiles and energies are very different.

— The hunter's profile

The biggest challenge for a hunter is making "cold calls" and turning them into positive relationships. As the risk for the company is high, their fixed salary should be low but the variable part should be quite important. The profile of the hunter will therefore be a sprinter rather than a long-distance runner. What they are looking for are quick results and a monthly bonus. They will be in an energy of conquest, challenge, optimism and will have a good stress tolerance.

I suggest hiring someone under 30 who is ambitious and doesn't yet have a large family to support. They can therefore take risks by accepting a low compensation package with a large variable portion. Another element, not to be underestimated, is travel. Whether in France, the USA, Vietnam or conquering new export markets, they will have to be willing to travel often and easily spend a third of their time away from home.

— The farmer's profile

Your first prospects are your customers! This is something that many companies forget. They are therefore surprised to see some leave each year. On the contrary, you know your customers and they know you and, most importantly, they trust you. So, you are already in a positive relationship.

That's why it's important that your business doesn't rest on its laurels and regularly launches new products or services. The easiest thing to do is to ask your customers about their unmet needs.

You therefore need a farmer sales profile. Their job will be to cultivate the relationship you have with your customers and to generate one way or another more business with them. Your sales rep should be very organized and technically sharp. Their salary package will be fixed with a less variable part. They will be in an energy of empathy and benevolence.

My suggestion is to hire someone who is at least 30 years old. They can of course be older. They already have a certain stable life as well as good professional experience. Since they will quickly get to know their customers, they can easily keep in touch with them via Zoom or a phone call, so they won't have to travel all the time. However, they must be professional and meticulous in following up with their clients. *"It takes years to build trust and a few seconds to destroy it"*.

Don't make the same mistake I made in the last company I ran. I had just taken over a small company together with a Private Equity. Our goal was to strongly develop this company internationally. After some market research, it turned out that there was very significant potential for us in West Africa. Our company had a senior salesperson who was going to retire in the next 3 years.

I made the mistake of combining the two profiles by hiring a 40-year-old senior salesperson (farmer) to lead the exploration of new markets (hunter) and replace the current salesperson when he retired. Can you guess the rest? He did not succeed at all in his first mission because he hardly ever left his office and he left us before he could replace the future retiree. So you see that even after so many years of experience, a CEO is still capable of making a significant recruiting mistake.

Management of sales teams

As the sales and marketing departments are the most strategic parts of your company, it is essential to manage their teams efficiently. Singularly, sales teams are also the most difficult to manage. There are three reasons for this.

The first is that salespeople are mostly out of office because they are supposed to be prospecting or serving customers. It is therefore essential to organize regular face-to-face or Zoom follow-up meetings.

The second is that a sales rep is someone who organizes their work and time as it suits them. In fact, it is the result that counts, not the hours worked. The discussions you have with them therefore focus on the current business they are managing and not on their schedule.

The third reason relates to the characteristics of the salesperson. They find energy in contacting people and not in reporting and figures. It is therefore essential that you have a CRM[1] type software in which they can easily file their reports and offers. At the same time, you will be able to track the information you are interested in without having to ask for it.

Internal and external sales network

Most of the sales networks of large corporations are made up of employees and managers. Managing these should not be too much of a problem.

However, most small and medium-sized companies do not have affiliates and use agents or distributors outside their home country. Many factors explain this: costs or lack of knowledge of these foreign markets. A mistake that many companies make is not to run their external network the same way they do their own salespeople. Of course, contractually and legally, we do not manage an agent or a distributor as we would with our own people. Indeed, these last two have several other non-competing brands in their portfolios.

The monitoring of agents and distributors is therefore different in its form but not in its substance. Regular contacts as well requesting weekly reporting from an agent or monthly reporting from a distributor contributes to the positive dynamics and cohesion of your network. All the agents and distributors I have known were themselves asking for a closer relationship with

---

1. CRM: *"Customer Relationship Management" manages interactions with potential as well as existing customers. It allows you to manage customer relationships by centralizing the information entered by your salespeople. It brings together all the services of your company in relation to prospects and customers, namely the sales, marketing, support, logistics, finance department, etc. It easily connects to the company's ERP. The most famous software in the world is Salesforce with a 20% market share.*

us. They also know much better than us the dynamics of their local market and its competitive landscape.

A healthy business starts with a good monitoring of its activity

There are plenty of CRM tools on the market, including Salesforce which is used worldwide. Yet no software, no matter how good, will replace good salesforce management.

In order to keep track and have a weekly discussion with your sales force or with your sales management, you can use a tool that I call the PIPELINE. Personally, in addition to all the CRM software, I use a small tool developed in Excel which is simple, and which has the merit of accurately predicting your future turnover. You can also use this tool for your annual budget because for each lead you have a deadline, a price and a probability. Below is an explanatory example.

Name Salesrep: Mr John Due				**PIPELINE**				DATE TODAY: 2021/03/08			
Project nb	Prospect name	Date first contact	Date last contact	Type of product or service	Potential Revenue 2021/2022 [USD]	% Target successrate	Adapted Revenue 2021/2022 [USD]	Target decision date	Target invoice date	Comments
1	**Prosp. 1**	20/09/19 170 days	21/02/19 17 days	Product XT	100 000 $	90 %	90 000 $	21/06/30	/	Pellentesque hendrerit id
2	**Prosp. 2**	20/10/21 138 days	21/01/29 38 days	Service FD	180 000 $	75 %	135 000 $	21/08/31	/	Etiam elent nisl mi tem
3	**Prosp. 3**	21/01/03 64 days	21/02/01 35 days	Product CG	500 000 $	50 %	250 000 $	21/09/30	/	Mauris frin mattis gravid
TOTAL					780 000 $		475 000 $			

The principle is quite simple: each sales manager asks each member of their team to discuss with their own sales reps the three most important ongoing business leads, their probable success rate and their targeted decision date. This will help you, as CEO, to have a clear view of your future business. In addition, you will have a good working document to discuss during your management meetings. As a result, your production manager, your purchasing manager and your logistics manager will be able to use this information to adapt their own planning as much as your financial manager for their financial projections.

The sales reps bonus plan

The bonus plan is the key element of any company in managing its commercial network. Through this plan, you are able to direct your salespeople. The most important thing is that the plan is in line with the needs of the corporation, and its profitability.

Below is an example of a bonus plan that I have been using for years.

1st principle:

The quantitative bonus must represent at least 80% of the total bonus and be able to be measured with indisputable figures such as the revenue achieved compared to the received target.

2nd principle:

The system must be fair. Below 70%, there will be no bonus. At 100% of the objectives achieved, the bonus will be 100%.

3rd principle:

If we exceed 100%, each point counts double. This is to motivate salespeople not to hide their December contracts in the drawer and bring them out in January the following year (a true story).

4th principle:

The bonus does not exceed 150%. Imagine that a national contract arrives in the territory of a salesperson and represents three years of his annual objective.

5th principle:

The qualitative bonus is used to measure objectives achieved when they cannot be quantified but can still be measured in one way or another (see below). You don't need more than three objectives. They can be linked to the list of progress points during the annual assessment. Here are a few: send your weekly report on time, fill out your client files adequately, involve your colleagues when a business is multizone, etc.

Annual bonus plan for sales representatives

BONUS

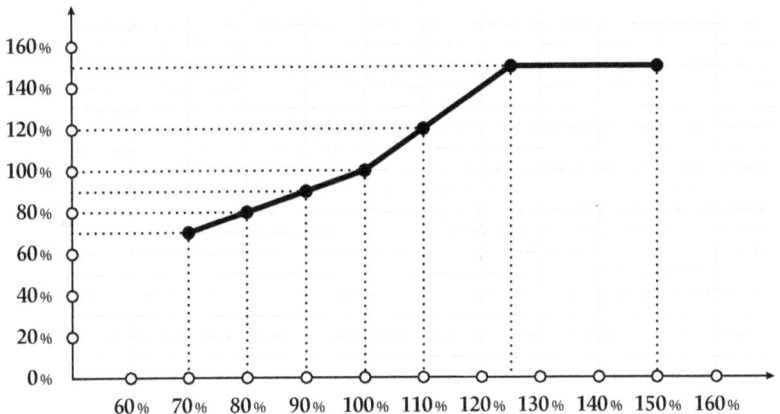

— **Quantitative Bonus : 80%**

Bonus is calculated at the beginning of January of the following year

- ∗ No bonus if below 70% of the quantitative target
- ∗ Percentage bonus between 70% & 100%
- ∗ Above 100%: 1% above target = 2% bonus
- ∗ Maximum quantitative bonus = 150%

— **Qualitative Bonus 20%**

Qualitative objectives

- ∗ Poor performance: 0%
- ∗ Normal performance: 50%
- ∗ Good performance: 70%
- ∗ Excellent performance: 100%

Salespeople are only judged on their results

There is a saying in life, it's only the result that counts. It's the same in business. Nothing is more frustrating for a CEO than to hear one of his staff say that it is not their fault that they did not achieve their goals, it's because of a new competitor, etc. When you are part of a company, you are linked for better and for worse. When the market explodes and all of the sales reps exceed 100% of their targets, none of them will tell you that their bonus is too high.

The same principle applies to your business meetings. Note in the meeting agenda that everything that is said must be quantified: such and such a prospect is interesting. OK but, what is his potential turnover? When will he make his decision? When is the next meeting scheduled, etc.? The sales reps are in principle not very structured: so be it for them.

The importance of language

The job of a salesperson is above all a job that involves emotion. The most common way to express emotion is through speech and therefore through language. Language translates the culture of people through its many expressions, some of which are hundreds of years old. I am personally fortunate to speak more than four languages. It is by being fluent in the language of others that you can really connect with their culture. In Europe and in Asia, multitudes of languages and dialects are spoken. My advice is simple. If you want your sales reps to be successful, and if you have the opportunity, hire them where possible to work in their region. It will therefore be a Texan in Texas, a New Yorker in New York, a north Vietnamese in Hanoi and a south Vietnamese in HCMC.

Let's party!

When a big contract is signed or when you've exceeded your yearly target, you have to celebrate. Not only between salespeople, but if possible, by inviting all the people who have contributed to the success.

— The bonus

If I ask you the question, what bonus did you receive in January five years ago? None of you will be able to answer me. You will only remember having to pay a lot of tax on it.

On the other hand, if your company covered all expenses for a trip for you and your partner for a weekend in Budapest, you will remember almost everything: the hotel, the restaurants, the bars, etc. Why does your brain hold back the one and not the other? Simply because a bonus paid into an account is emotionless whereas a trip gives you plenty of emotions, and that's something your brain will remember.

— The trip

When I was CEO of Fountain and business at the time was booming, I had the idea of organizing a trip to Morocco for all my reps. Their only contribution was to arrive on a specific date at Zaventem airport in Belgium. On D-Day, 120 people from several different countries gathered at the airport. I had chartered a plane that would take us to Ouarzazate (a town in southern Morocco) followed by a road trip to Marrakech. I had planned a stopover in the middle of the desert where we would all sleep in Berber tents, after spending the evening around a barbecue. When we arrived in Marrakech, we had everything prepared for the launch of our new products. The next day, the return plane was waiting for us.

While relations with our reps had been difficult for years, this trip allowed us to get to know each other from a new perspective. We also had several sales reps with us from our various affiliates. These few days filled with emotion and unforgettable memories allowed us to strengthen the cohesion of our company and facilitated the sale of our new product offer launched in Marrakech. In addition, all those present, employees and customers, felt unanimously that this trip had been a sign of gratitude for them. And that was priceless!

A few months later, I reviewed this trip with my CFO. The margins generated by the additional sales made as a result of our renewed offer had already offset 50% of the total cost of the trip. The rest would be recovered easily over the following months.

Don't forget to party with your staff and with your customers! It will give everyone an energy boost! It will bring a sense of cohesion and ultimately cost you less than signing hard-won contracts with your clients or losing key executives to the competition due to a stagnant office atmosphere.

CHAPTER 4
My relationship with external stakeholders

A company does not live in dictatorship, it also has external stakeholders. These are the shareholders, customers, suppliers, unions and bankers. When you are CEO, it is important to have good personal contact with all these stakeholders.

The shareholders and the Board of Directors

— The company's equity

Without shareholders, there would be no companies. Many employees, workers and sometimes even unions forget this. However, it is the shareholders, large or small, who one day put their money in a company in order to start or to develop it. It is therefore normal that they are also the ultimate decision makers. The only downside I would add is that shareholders also have a moral and civic responsibility. There is no business without the men and women who keep the business running smoothly. Shareholders have a de facto responsibility to respect these people for whom wages are generally the only source of income.

I respect all those people who have invested a large part of their assets in a business to make it grow. They take a risk and carry on their lives with the threat, though unlikely, of losing everything one day, due to unforeseeable external factors such as COVID-19.

— Alignment

We are complex human beings and we do not always have the same interests. This is why it's so important to be clear on which direction to take. In this case, alignment means putting the different aspects of our subjective experience at the service for the same purpose: namely the success of the company.

How to achieve this in practice? By being transparent with peers in every direction and by keeping them regularly informed. Don't we say out of sight out of mind? Do the exercise on your own. Prepare a list of people around you at the office who you talk to on a regular basis, for example, once or twice a week. Then prepare a list of those you rarely talk to, at most once a month. Now prepare a list of the people who are key to your day-to-day job or to your career. Normally the names on the first and third lists should match. If not, it's time to change your habits.

For a CEO, it is fundamental to be aligned and transparent with your management team. However, over time, I realize that it is almost more fundamental that the vision of the shareholder is shared on a regular basis with that of the CEO.

In fact, to have good "management/shareholder" alignment, there is often a third element to consider: the Board of Directors and its chairman.

> **The shareholders** delegate the management of the company to a Board of Directors, which reports each year at an Annual General Meeting (AGM).

> **The Board of Directors** decides on the strategy and approves the budget, generally on the basis of the proposals made by the CEO; the Board then delegates execution to the CEO.

> **The CEO** executes the decided strategy and reports to the Board of Directors on the results obtained; to this end, he himself delegates many responsibilities to his management team and / or to his employees.

Shareholders	*Delegate the management of the company*
President & Board of directors	*Delegate the execution of the strategy and the budget*
CEO	*Delegate the operations*
Departements	

Suppliers

The quality and price of the products that we put on the market depend primarily on the quality of our suppliers. What are the essential elements that you should look for in each of your suppliers?

* **Sustainability**
    → Your supplier cannot disappear overnight

* **Product**
    → Your supplier must constantly assure you of a quality defined by you

* **Profitability**
    → The price / quality ratio must be equal to or better than the market

* **Delivery**
    → Your supplier must respect the promised and confirmed delivery time

* **Technology**
    → Your supplier must inform you of any technological improvements affecting the quality or the price of the product

* **Alternatives**
    → Your supplier should be replaceable in the medium term

The purchasing department therefore has a strong responsibility to be constantly on the alert. They must ensure that the points listed above are respected at all times. But their biggest enemy could be their ego because they will always be flattered by their suppliers. It is therefore important to distinguish between purchasing and procurement.

The act of purchase is unique and / or usually annual. It includes a multitude of legal clauses of which the price and delivery times are the most important elements. Your purchasing manager therefore bears a great responsibility because he commits your company at several levels. That's why, as CEO, I have always asked to sign major purchase agreements myself when they were previously negotiated. This mutually forced us to carefully analyse the content and allowed us to avoid any misunderstandings in the event of problems later.

Procurement is carried out in each department involved with production, taking into account lead times and this in a reasonable manner. You have to find the right balance. You must always have enough stock to ensure production, but you must also avoid surplus which would be linked to an attractive promotion and which would lead to an overstock and unnecessarily blocked financial resources.

I have often wanted to meet my suppliers outside of negotiation periods. I have always considered them partners. For their part, they provided me with a wealth of information on the market and its development, on my competitors, on the new products that would arrive in the future, etc. The vast majority of my suppliers told me that it was rare for them to have the opportunity to speak to the CEO. However, they should not try to bypass my purchasing department during the annual negotiation period. Every man to his trade!

— Suppliers and mutual respect

Being CEO of an SME, I encountered suppliers that were ten or a hundred times the size of my company. I was often struck by their arrogance and inflexibility. The most frustrating time was when a sales rep told me about a price increase or a discontinuation of a particular product without previously refusing the decision of my supplier.

Once in my career, I braved a large coffee multinational who, following a new production technology, wanted to force me to put their logo on my products. Along with my purchasing manager, in secret, we visited several alternative suppliers. Once we'd decided on the most promising, we started to do the taste and smell tests for each possibility. Then, we asked two distributors, one in France and the other in the Netherlands, to distribute three of their flagship products without mentioning anything to anyone. Once we were sure that the risk of having customer complaints was minimal, I took the matter to the Board of Directors for approval. Six months later, we withdrew 80% of our references from this multinational by transferring them to another supplier. The cherry on the cake was that our purchase prices fell on average by more than 40%. We shared part of the profits with our distributors, but this case also had a positive impact of 15% on our EBITDA for that year.

The moral of this story is that you should always respect the little guys, whether they are customers or suppliers. Because one needs the other and vice versa. And... don't forget to pay the small suppliers first because they need the cash flow the most.

The customers

— The four golden rules

For my part, there are four golden rules to know and respect regarding customers:

* The money in my wallet comes from my client.
* The valuation of a company results from the quality of its customers.
* A customer must be heard and respected.
* A customer pays his bills, otherwise he's not a customer.

If everyone in your company agrees with these four rules, you will have a healthy business.

The first rule is simple. As my client is my bread and butter, I look after them, I respect him, I make sure to keep him for a long time. The fourth rule is also clear.

The second rule is less obvious because it does not appear in the reports used by management.

What is a quality customer? It's someone who has bought a product that perfectly meets their needs. How many salespeople, to ensure their bonus, sell a product that they know in advance is not suitable for their customer or that their customer does not have the creditworthiness to pay for it. What will happen then?

* The customer is ultimately not satisfied with the product and you will find it out at your expense and put it back in your stock as a second-hand product with 30% reduced value.
* The customer does not pay his bills. After spending time recuperating unpaid bills and going to court, you will either recuperate some or none of it back.
* The client goes bankrupt. Then you are sure to have lost everything.

Besides the risk of loss of value, you will also lose brand image. What do you think this dissatisfied customer will tell his colleagues when they talk about your business and your products?

I return to this customer who bought one of your products and who is very satisfied with it. This client will be:

* Your first prospect, because he will be ready to welcome you if you have something else to offer him that might be of interest.

* Your first salesperson, because he will be proud of his purchase and will talk about it with his friends and acquaintances.

* Your asset, because they will be there for a long time and will decrease your annual percentage of customer churn (attrition).

— Connecting the dots

After all these years as CEO, I really enjoyed my customer's visits and most importantly, I learned so much.

When you are the boss of an SME, you sometimes learn things that seem anecdotal, but which can have major consequences on the good or bad perception of the quality of your products.

When I was CEO of Fountain, I regularly visited our clients in France, Belgium, the Netherlands and Denmark. It was through these visits that I noticed big differences in the use of our coffee machines.

In France, coffee is a social drink: we meet around the coffee machine to chat. Often the coffee is small and served in a plastic or cardboard cup. In order not to burn your tongue, the coffee must therefore come out of the machine at a temperature below 80°.

In the Netherlands and Denmark, coffee is considered a source of energy. Everyone will therefore help themselves to a coffee in a large mug and go back to their office. If the coffee does not come out at 95° from the machine, it will be lukewarm a few minutes later. So, it was important to have machines in stock that were pre-set at the right temperature and had the right outlet pipe. Indeed, you cannot imagine the number of complaints received by the network about the incorrect temperature of the coffee or the wrong choice of outlet...

The CEO is the only person in a company who is fortunate enough to be exposed to all facets of his company. He is therefore also responsible for grouping information together: "connecting the dots". Indeed, the technician in Denmark will tell the customer whose machine is overflowing that there has been an error at the factory and that it is not the right pipe. He will not know that this pipe is intended for machines in France. I am giving you this real-life story to make you smile. Be sure that you will encounter the same type of situation when you visit your customers. When you return, you will be able to discuss with your R&D or production managers in order to make the necessary improvements.

— The right attitude: listening and respect

The third rule is about listening and respect. The right attitude to have as a CEO towards your customers is not to promote your business but to listen to what your customer has to say. Your sales rep's task is to talk about your company and sell your products. Your mission is to listen to, question, and respect your client's message.

I remember leaving a customer visit having had an exchange with the salesperson and hearing him say: "Strange, he never told me that before!" Normal, your presence puts the customer in another energy. He feels valued by your listening and is happy to provide you with lots of relevant information. On the other hand, respect your customer's message. Don't interrupt him with a "yes but". His message is inevitably subjective, but don't we say that perception is reality?

Trade unions

Any corporation with a certain number of employees is bound to face one or more trade union. Their role is to ensure the collective and individual defence of the interests of your employees, at a company level but also at a national level. I have personally come into contact with trade unions in several companies that I managed. I have to admit that I have mixed memories of them. Sometimes I have found myself facing charming personalities, very professional in their approach and attitudes, and in other cases I have faced the exact opposite. My general conclusion is that, as in any human relationship, there are factors that make the difference, such as personalities, egos, competence, and the interdependence of the representative or trade union representative.

Here are four tips that I especially reserve for CEOs:

— Keep a cool head

During my first weeks as CEO at AMP, a press distributor with 1,200 employees, my HR Director visited with a pamphlet distributed by a trade union organization to all the company's staff. The slogan read: "Is there a pilot in the plane?" It was their welcome gift to the new CEO. The advice of my HRD was not to react but to organize meetings in small groups to clearly explain the group's strategy and to answer questions.

I cannot count how many strike threats I experienced during my time at AMP. As the leading newspaper distributor in Belgium and since the online press was still in its early years, we were easy prey for disruptors who wanted to show off. Fortunately, during all my time as a CEO, I was able to abort any strike within the first few hours: all the newspapers were delivered on time to kiosks. Of course, I won't tell you how many times I was woken up at night to go into the field.

— Don't put yourself on the front line

The CEO-trade union relationship is very ambiguous. On the one hand, you need to have personal contact with their leaders, and on the other hand, you need to keep a distance so that you don't get caught in the crossfire. So, let your HRD manage the works council meetings and the many mini conflicts. That's their role. Give them free rein and decide when it's time for you to intervene.

— Maintain a good relationship with trade union leaders

For any CEO, it is essential to maintain a good relationship with trade union leaders for the good reason that in the event of a crisis, you need direct contact with them on your smartphone.

Personally, the meetings I had with trade union leaders often took place in a restaurant. This allowed us to get to know each other better, to respect each other and above all to create a human relationship despite the fact that we were in a power struggle. It also allowed me to develop some "best practices" between us.

— Protect the first level of management

In order to achieve their ends as effectively as possible, trade union representatives will always try to have direct contact with the decision-maker of any company and will readily bypass all intermediate levels. It's a fair game. They will also inform their base very quickly as soon as they have important information. Your role is to make sure that your first level of management is informed by its hierarchy before the base is informed by the unions. Indeed, nothing is more frustrating for a supervisor than to learn from their subordinates a decision concerning the entity for which they are responsible.

Bankers

Bankers play a vital role in any business. They are there when a growing company needs to finance its working capital[1].

Bankers are also present when a company decides to develop itself through external acquisitions or needs money for a huge investment in its production facility.

If the client-banker relationship had to be summed up in one word, I would choose the word "trust".

Bankers often take risks by lending you money. Unlike mortgages where they have a building as collateral, their other loans are often based on business plans with covenants[2].

Personally, I have always had a great relationship with my bankers. Even today, they still trust me. My motto has always been the same: I say what I do, and I do what I say.

My advice is to always maintain a good relationship with your bankers even in times when you don't need them. They have good memories. Be transparent and communicate with them regularly. Be sure of it, a day will come when you will need their help.

---

1. WC: Working capital relates to the money the company permanently needs to finance its operations. It's the cash needed in its day-to-day trading operations, calculated as the current assets minus the current liabilities.

2. Covenants: safeguard clauses; these are conditions built into a loan agreement. They define the borrower's different commitments. These clauses can lead to early repayment of the loan in the event of failure to meet the objectives.

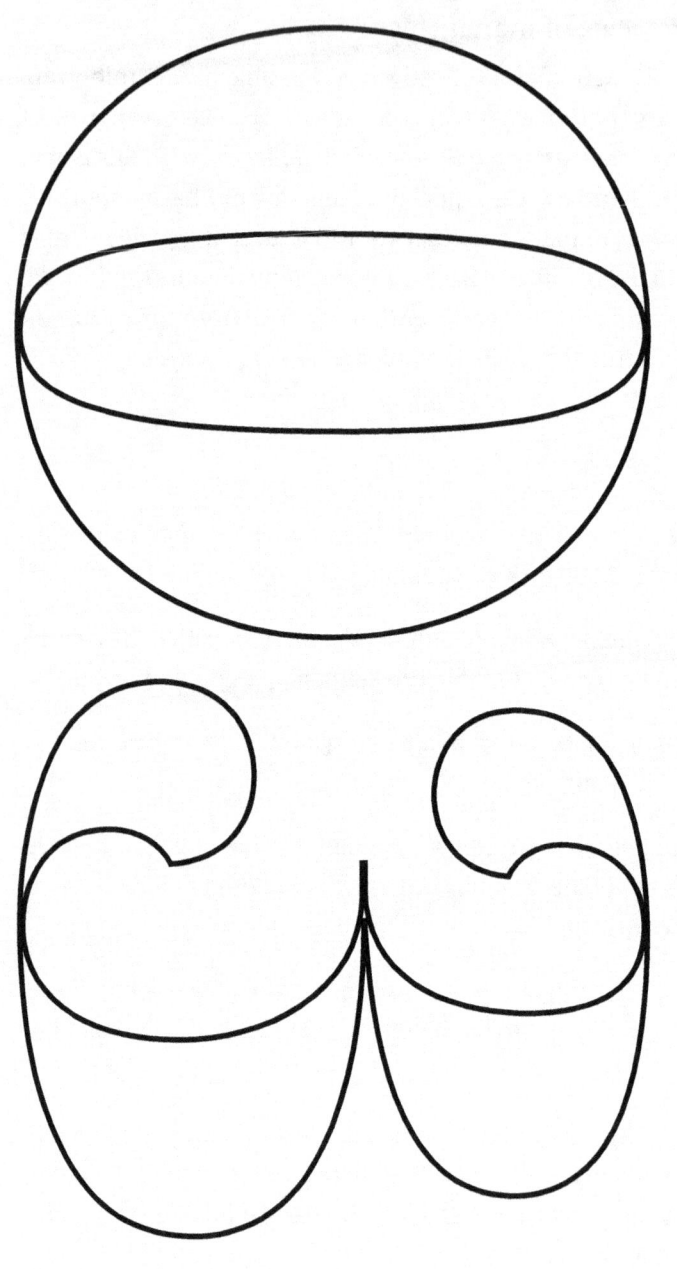

CORPORATE CHALLENGES

For human life to emerge, cells must multiply. The secret of life therefore lies in growth, expansion and movement. Day alternates with night, inhales with exhales. Even seemingly calm water is always oxygenated by underground movement. A tree grows because its roots anchor it to the ground, absorbing water and nutrients, and because its leaves, through photosynthesis, provide the energy it needs. A business also has a vocation to grow. It's natural.

CHAPTER 1
Internal growth

Growth is a natural thing

Look at the natural world around you... What do you see when you walk in an orchard or in the woods? You see trees. What other creation in nature symbolizes life better than a tree? Year after year, its growth never stops. A tree that does not grow is a dead tree. The same rule is true for us, human beings. From our birth to our death. In our personal life as in our professional life. We go from project to project and that gives us energy. A man who has no more plans is a dead man. The same is true for a business.

The life cycle of a company

— The growth

A company is made up of people. Like them, their company must grow. If you have an open mindset, life will push you forward with incredible energy. If we look beyond the human and philosophical aspect and do a simple economic calculation, we see the financial benefit that growth brings with it.

As the graph below illustrates, when a company is growing, profits grow faster than costs. This is easily explained by the fact that growing your business does not automatically increase your fixed costs such as your rent, administrative costs, salaries for your management team.

As the Law of Attraction states: *Success attracts success.*

GROWTH

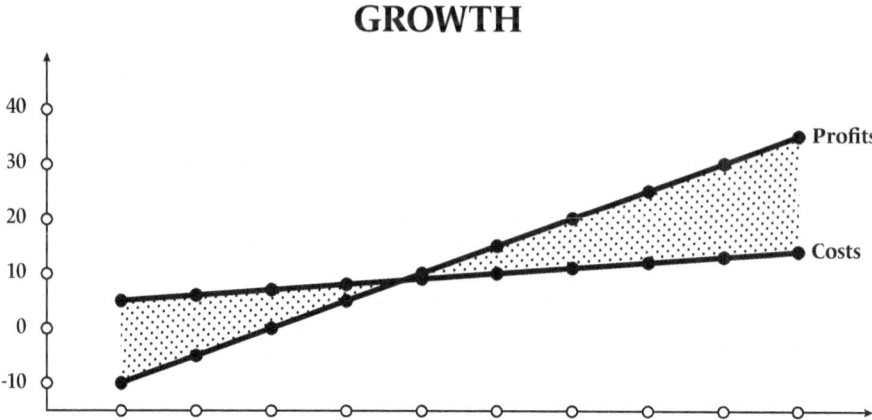

— The decline

A company without projects is a company that will one day experience a decline and then disappear.

Internal factors

Three internal factors can explain a decrease of a business.

1. The management

Sluggish management, too safe in their comfort zone, can be an internal factor of decline. Not seeing the evolution of the market around them, they are in a closed mindset. They are anchored in their past successes and naively believe that the future will be a carbon copy of what they have already known. This is the phenomenon of habit and passivity in an environment that is gradually deteriorating to the point of endangering the life of the company.

Without a wake-up call, the story of the frog can be repeated over and over again. If you immerse it in cold water and very gradually bring the water to a boil, the frog will go numb and eventually die. This story reflects a common phenomenon that I experienced when I joined a company as a new CEO; namely that if you don't react, you will inevitably get bogged down. The role of a new CEO is therefore to create the necessary boost to re-mobilize management around a new vision, a new project.

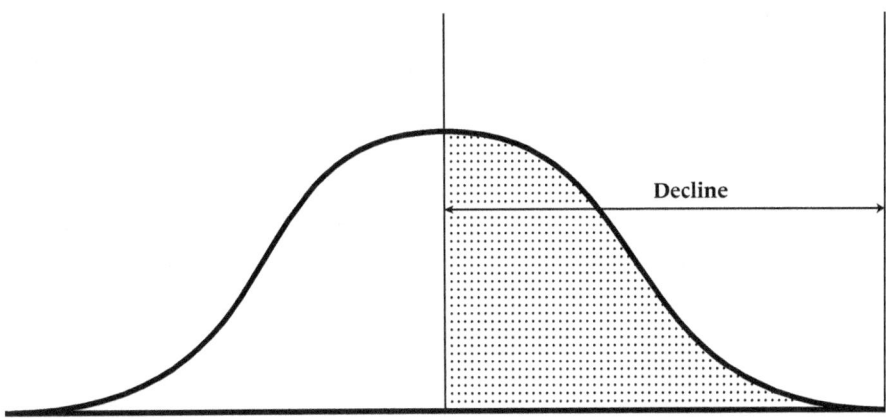

2. The product

Your product's value proposition erodes over time. Consumption habits change little by little, even if your customer base is stable and your product is highly appreciated. Gradually, your natural loss of customers will not be replaced by newcomers.

Even if the production tool is well depreciated, your marketing budget is reduced to zero and the profitability of your product or service is good, erosion slowly increases until the moment when, suddenly, it's too late to react.

3. The price

All European and American companies experienced this dilemma in the 1990s and early 2000s; their cost price was simply becoming too high and their margins were melting like snow in the sun. Here and there, a competitor took the initiative to relocate its production to countries with lower overheads. Others simply decided to outsource their production to focus on sales and marketing. In a very short time, this wave of offshoring and outsourcing turned into a tsunami. Even before management could react, it was already too late. Their offer, and therefore their company, was out of the market, and therefore doomed to die.

External factors

Sometimes you're the CEO of a very profitable, growing business in a changing industry and all of a sudden, in a matter of months or years, you are dead meat. Three factors are the major sources of this situation.

1. Disruption

The COVID-19 pandemic has reminded us that in a very short period of time, anything can happen and erase years of work. I don't remember having read anything about the Spanish flu that struck the world between 1918 and 1920. Yet, there are a lot of similarities between these two periods. As a CEO, it is difficult to predict any disruptive event. However, when you are developing your strategic plan, I suggest that you work on different scenarios and include one that foresees the unforeseeable.

2. Technology

A lot of people say that technology is the cause of this or that. On the contrary, technology has never revolutionized the world in itself. Instead, technology made things possible in order to meet the underlying expectations of men on this earth. Who has never dreamed of choosing a product from his sofa and having it home delivered within 24 hours? Who has never dreamed of instantly sharing unforgettable moments with their friends while being separated from them?

3. Purchasing and consumer habits

Like it or not, our buying habits and bank payments change over time, and are more pronounced from one generation to another. So, depending on what industry you are in, look into the buying habits of your customers. Even in B2B, buying habits are changing drastically. So, don't rest on your laurels!

The 4 keys to successful internal growth

When I look at companies that have had successful organic growth, I notice one thing: they have a unique product or service that is difficult to copy. If you look at Tesla, Apple, Samsung, Huawei, Netflix, Salesforce, WordPress and Zoom, you will see that it is above all the originality of their offer that makes them grow and not their sales or marketing forces.

— Client centricity

The first thing to do is to make sure that your *Value Proposition*[1] meets your client's expectations. Gone are the days of imposing your product on future customers through big budget advertising. Today, consumers have endless ways to find the product they are looking for via the Internet. We no longer impose anything on them, however we inform them.

— To be better than your competitor

Two tourists walking unarmed in the bush suddenly see a lion coming their way in search of a good meal. One of the two immediately opens his bag and begins to put on his sneakers. "You're crazy," said the other, "Do you think you can run faster than the lion?" "Of course not, but I would like to run faster than you".

The moral of this story is that you don't have to have the best product or service in the world. It would be priceless, and no one would buy it. You simply have to be better than your competitors in terms of price/quality.

— To work in project mode

I have often noticed that many companies have departments that work in silos without any smooth and effective interaction between them.

It is the role of the CEO to ensure that any launch of a new product should be handled in the form of project management. This means that we bring together members of R&D, production, marketing and sales in a project team with a clear objective: to successfully launch a product, or service on time that will correspond to the demand and to the needs of the customer. I will develop the methodology in a specific chapter later in this book.

— Funding for new products and services

It's often difficult for companies to launch new products or services. The top management asks their teams for a good business plan with solid profit at the end. Because of this, a lot of great projects will never see the light of day. You should know that successful businesses work differently. They use the cash generated by their "cash cow" products to finance new projects in which

---

1. *The Value Proposition (VP) is a phrase that clearly explains to your customer what benefits they will have by purchasing your product or service, how it will solve or improve their situation and what its specific advantages are. It is present on your website or in your physical shops and in the language of your target customer.*

they believe. These projects can then be loss-making for a few years, but many of them will ensure the future profitability for their entire business.

Different types of internal growth

— Innovation

It's no mystery that the most innovative companies grow the fastest. I will not dwell on this subject, but you should know that innovating does not mean bringing a revolutionary product or service to market. When this is the case, the company has often had to find funds from private investors with deep pockets. I am thinking of groups like Tesla, Uber or Airbnb.

Other types of innovation that are more accessible to your business exist. Among dozens of possibilities, I mention, for example, incremental innovations such as new collections or new product designs, or new manufacturing processes. The latter make it possible, with few industrial resources, to launch products aimed at new markets.

— Differentiation

When I arrived as CEO of a company specialized in barbecues, we sold our products through a traditional distribution network as well as through online platforms. This classic method required the storage of a wide range of products. The difficulty was not only to develop new designs but place orders to our subcontractors in China. The other real issue was to order enough sock so as not to run out while making sure not to end up with too many unsold items at the end of the season. Indeed, the cost of storage is important as well as the cost of depreciation of unsold stock.

During a brainstorming session, we decided to launch a range of in & out products. The idea was to go to our distributors and offer them, in addition to our normal range, a reduced selection of products at an attractive price but with the obligation to purchase by full container and without a return policy.

Being able to manufacture large batches, to deliver them directly and without having to worry about stocking them, allowed us to experience strong growth in our sales that year while keeping a good profit margin.

The products were virtually the same as our classic range, but the way of producing, selling and distributing them was innovative.

— New markets and segments

It is also possible for you in certain cases, with your production tool, to manufacture, without significant additional costs, a new range of products aimed at a new market segment. That was the case when I joined a company specialized in the sale of canned ready meals and hotdogs. We noticed that there was a growing niche in the market: for halal food products. We therefore decided to market a new range of hotdogs with a halal label. In order to sell our chicken hotdogs with the halal label, we had to considerably adapt our manufacturing process. We also had to obtain certification from a recognized body. A little less than a year after the start of our project, a new product range could be brought to a new market segment that was previously unknown to us.

— Export

For many companies, exports are smoke and mirrors.

As a rule, when the home market of a company is saturated, it opens up to new markets in order to strengthen its growth.

Some companies seek growth at all costs and immediately establish themselves in several countries at the same time. This happens quite often in the IT and telecommunications sectors.

Sometimes companies, not happy with their success in their home market, set their sights on exporting, hoping to find the holy grail.

My advice is very simple. Don't try to fill another pool until you have filled your own. Having lived and worked in three continents myself, I am well placed to have known and experienced all the cultural differences that exist from one country to another. These differences are huge, especially when it comes to culinary products.

Another mistake that many companies make is not taking the easy route. It happens that after an international trade fair, entrepreneurs have new contacts and in a very short time receive order forms in a foreign language from the other side of the world. The salesperson who instigated this new business is very proud. He is even invited by his new customer to come and visit him. However, the factory manager is tearing his hair out because the product's certificates are not suited to this particular country. It is therefore necessary to be audited by a new body and possibly adapt the manufacturing process. The marketing director is not happy because they have to change the packaging and translate everything related to the product into a new language, not to mention the user manual.

Of course, the website must also be amended, etc. Next comes the logistics manager who asks you to sell only by full container, etc.

So, if you are the CEO of an SME, be extremely careful before exporting. Pay attention to at least the following:

1. If you are a small company and new to exporting, choose a country that speaks the same language as you. France will therefore be the ideal choice for any French-speaking Belgian company, an English-speaking country a British company, a Spanish speaking country for a Spanish company. You will then have virtually no additional costs for marketing, manufacturing and storage.

2. I also recommend exporting to neighboring countries first. For Belgium it would therefore be France, Germany, Luxembourg and the Netherlands. This will have the advantage that all transport of goods will be done by truck. In addition, it will be easy for you to set up a network of agents and distributors with whom you can then meet regularly.

3. Don't start major exporting before having a competent sales staff within your company with the appropriate marketing, industrial, logistical and financial monitoring tools.

4. For any agent or distributor contract, have it drafted by a lawyer specialized in your business. The biggest danger is using standard contracts. Personally, I had the chance to work with an exceptional lawyer, Christine D., who explained that for each contract clause, you had to choose between several options, some more favorable to the distributor, others more favorable towards us. The tricky thing was to find the

right middle ground for both parties. One particular clause, the contract termination clause, remains the most complicated and requires much attention as it is subject to the law of each country.

The effectiveness of internal growth

Sometimes companies don't have an offer in their portfolio that really stands out from their competitors. One example is when you are operating in the services sector.

That was precisely the case with a company I ran. It provided 50,000 customers with coffee machines. Almost all of the coffee machines that we delivered to our customers were purchased from Italian manufacturers. We serviced them with coffee on a regular basis and provided the maintenance of their machines. Our differentiation then played out practically only on service and price. Our slogan was "Service first" at the time, doesn't it make sense?

Our salespeople aimed to find 12 new customers per month so that their salary would be repaid after 18 months. As some of them did not meet their targets and others left us, the cost of acquiring each customer became an issue. It was therefore quite difficult for us to experience profitable growth. However, we put great effort into achieving operational excellence. This translated into a great customer experience together with irreproachable maintenance service. Imagine a coffee machine breaking down for more than a day! This excellence was our USP and it allowed us to be recognized as a reliable player in the market. Our revenue growth was then obtained through acquisitions of local distributors, and therefore through external growth.

Operational excellence does not create rapid growth but helps reduce the erosion of your customer base. In fact, you are securing an extremely loyal customer base who could also be your first sales rep. Indeed, a satisfied customer will promote your product and your company for free.

CHAPTER 2
External growth

We saw in the previous chapter that internal growth is not always a universal remedy and that, in certain circumstances, external growth is more suited to the success of a company's strategic plan. Any strategic growth plan is usually presented to the Board of Directors. Like any plan, the central question will be: "What is the ROI[1] of this plan?"

Different reasons lead companies to move towards external growth rather than internal growth.

When the cost of growing in a saturated market is too high

In Western Europe, most companies are faced with a saturated market. Usually, when you win a new customer, it's to the detriment of a competitor. At the microeconomic level, commercial costs have been incurred to achieve zero enrichment. A price war sets in and everyone ends up losing.

When the financial risk is too high

I attended dozens of budget meetings during my years as CEO. Very often the plans presented to me were very attractive. Then we took our calculator. One thing was certain: the required growth budget was going to be spent. What was much less sure, was the success rate of new business related to the costs incurred.

---

1. *ROI: Return on Investment*

When the time of organic growth is too long

You all know the expression: "Time is money". Developing a new product or a new market takes time. Your engineers are obviously very proud and very motivated to work on new projects. Do you know any product or market development project that has landed on time? Personally, I think I can count them on the fingers of one hand. The problem is that you are not alone in the market and competition is expanding too.

In the three cases I just mentioned, external growth is much more suitable. Some companies have understood this well, especially in the digital world. By focusing on external growth, you can, under specific circumstances, gain three times your growth speed. Alphabet, the parent company of Google bought 66 companies between 2015 and 2020. In 2010 and 2011, Google bought a company every two weeks.

When external growth has two secrets

I see around me a lot of beautiful European companies who believe they have to make acquisitions in the USA rather than focusing on their European market. I'm sure the CEO's ego must have had something to do with it. These acquisitions are rarely profitable and sometimes even turn into nightmares. But the biggest danger is not just money spent without success. The danger comes from elsewhere. All the energy of the Board of Directors goes to another continent. We send our best executives there to fix the situation and during that time, we leave a managerial vacuum in our own market. Here it is, a blessing for local competitors!

Two golden rules to remember.

— We only buy healthy businesses that we know well

Do you know your geographical environment or your sector well? Don't move out of it.

Look for companies in your area even if they are not in your immediate vicinity. Make sure these acquisitions aren't too far apart and can easily fit into your existing network. When I arrived at Fountain as the new CEO, my predecessors had bought a distributor in the Czech Republic. It was great fun going there but this acquisition was in a small country with no possibility of integration or economies of scale. On the other hand, it fell within my scope of consolidation and required assiduous managerial follow-up in order to ensure its financial viability. Two years after my arrival, I was able to resell it to a local company who simply joined my international independent network of resellers.

On the other hand, in the years that followed, I made several acquisitions in France where I was already present with subsidiaries. The synergies were therefore obvious between them.

— One plus one equals three

As we already were present in France, it was easy for us to purchase several of our independent distributors. Since we had just made an IT migration to SAP, it was possible for us to manage inventory centrally.

This translated into better purchasing conditions and less need for working capital by avoiding excess inventory. Our administration could also be centralized as well as certain services such as telesales.

These acquisitions also enabled us to win national tenders which required a uniform level of pricing and service throughout the country.

Do your maths before buying a company. Above all, pay attention to a successful integration into your network, to the synergies that this acquisition can bring to you in terms of the reciprocity of your offer as well as to the savings that it can bring to your cost structure.

When you have to choose between internal or external growth

I hope it's clear for you now, there are no standard rules for favoring one form of growth over another. Each company, each sector, each market and each region is specific.

 * Calculate the cost of acquiring a new customer for your business and see the best solution for yourself.

* Take into account the speed of growth of a market as well as the time required to develop your product.
* Stay open to both solutions and do not be dogmatic in your choices.

When the value of a business is linked to its growth

You will have noticed that high growth companies sometimes have stock market valuations that make you dream. When you see that in February 2021, Tesla's P/E[1] is 1330, Google's is 35 and BMW's is 13, there is a lot to wonder about, right? In fact, the higher the P / E, the greater the expected profit growth of a company in the future. Why?

If someone is interested in buying your business, that person will look at your past performance, but more importantly they will calculate the future profits that could be generated if the growth continues at the same rate in the years to come. The prospective acquirer will therefore be inclined to pay more if the company experiences strong growth rather than an average growth or no growth at all.

When you need to know it's time to stop

Sometimes if you fail, you need to have the courage to abandon a development strategy before the costs threaten your business. Unfortunately, it was too late for Crédit Lyonnais in 1993 or for Fortis in 2008.

In your company, there can also be times when a growth strategy turns into a horror story.

Sometimes, you hire a manager for one of your divisions who promises you wonders with a very ambitious but very expensive business plan.

The first year they crash: sales have not increased. They have excuses. Let's give them a little more time because you will see what you will see in the second year! Again, the following year, disappointing results. In the meantime,

---

1. *P/E: The price-earnings ratio is calculated by dividing market capitalization by net income, or by dividing the price of a share by the net income per share.*

your company's cash flow is shrinking and melting like snow in the sun. So, don't wait any longer to replace them. I call these managers the hockey stick specialists. Each year they promise miracles, but the following year they are still at the same point as the year before.

Growth

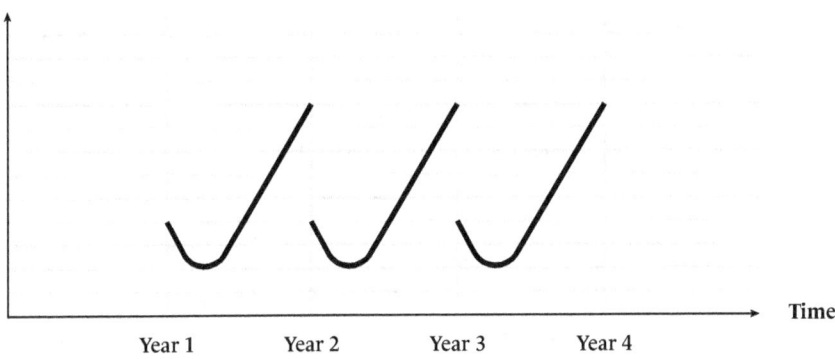

The story I tell you happens more often than you think. In retrospect, you wonder how this could have been possible? Why didn't we act sooner? The reason is often to be found in the ego of the manager, the leader or the members of the Board of Directors who did not want to question themselves at the time.

When rapid expansion is also risky

In its life cycle, a company can sometimes experience very rapid growth for various reasons. At first glance, this may seem good. If this happens to you, I send you my congratulations. However, your role as CEO is not only to guide and manage but also to plan. Often, fast growing companies have an organization that fails to adapt in a timely way.

There are three types of risks:

— Your backoffice

Rapid growth in your sales requires careful monitoring of your support services. Often, your IT tool is no longer suitable. Order errors are on the rise, as are billing errors. Payment of your invoices by your customers are less well monitored. In short, your management tools are no longer suitable for the new challenges and size of your business. Your margins and profit don't follow the same trend as your sales, and you wonder why. Do not wait for problems to arise, nor for it to be too late to invest quickly in the appropriate management tools.

— Your staff

You started your company with a small, motivated team. Everyone knew each other. In the evening after work, you went for a drink as a team and the little brawls of the day were discussed and resolved. You didn't feel the need for reporting or weekly meetings. The informal communication within your small group was adequate because everyone knew each other.

And then comes the day when the decision is made to hire new staff because you are riding the growth wave. You therefore hire new salespeople, administrative staff, technicians, etc. Little by little, the atmosphere, which was great at the start, is not the same. New people do their job badly: they don't understand what to do and complain about not receiving training or coaching. The original staff complain that they always have to explain everything and fix the mistakes of the new ones. Everyone is complaining that they are not aware of what is going on in the company.

Do not panic, what is happening is quite normal! You don't run a company of 50 or 100 people like a company of 20. A growing company must adapt its mode of operation while keeping its core values. If this ever happens to you, in order to save time, I recommend that you hire executives who come from larger companies than yours. They will naturally put in place the tools and methods essential for your growing company.

— Cash

The biggest challenge for any rapidly growing company is always having enough cash to pay the bills. Monitoring your WCR (working capital requirement) is therefore essential. In fact, in order to be able to follow demand, you increase your purchases with your suppliers. Your customers, however, will not pay for the goods you produced until much later. It is therefore essential that you have a close relationship with your bankers or with your investors and that you have your cash forecast ready for the next three months. Too many companies have gone bankrupt when they were becoming successful.

Their debt ratio was probably too high, they could no longer borrow more to finance their growth, or they had insufficient equity. So never forget the maxim: CASH IS KING!

CHAPTER 3
Business in transition

You have probably known a company within your professional network that has taken initiatives to improve its efficiency or to solve key problems. This company probably also had to make changes to its processes and organization. This is called Change Management.

From vision to transition

When a company appoints a new CEO, following an acquisition or a change of generation, their Board of Directors will surely ask the question: where do we want to be in five years?

It will be the role of the CEO to present them with a vision. Once accepted, it will be clearly communicated internally in order to mobilize and motivate the staff to follow their leader in their vision and the accompanying objectives.

The vision will then be set out in a strategic plan which itself will result in a roadmap. Often, the company will need loans and / or a capital increase to finance its plan. All parts of the company as well as stakeholders will therefore be affected by this ambitious project.

Change must be a state of mind in your company

The world around us is disruptive. The arrival of new technologies and new consumer habits is forcing companies to adapt or disappear. The arrival of COVID-19 has further accelerated the phenomenon. If our current world is in perpetual motion, it is normal that companies seize the opportunities that arise. As organizations are made up of women and men, it is important that each person is infused with a mindset that makes them feel comfortable with change in all its forms. I have the impression that the Millennials have this mindset. Unfortunately, the other generations that make up the current management of companies don't always see things the same way. It is therefore essential that any change be accompanied by a clear and well-organized roadmap in order to minimize the stress caused by the unknown.

Change Management

— The main reasons for failure of change management

Did you know that approximately 70% of change programs fail to meet their goals? Do you know why? The three reasons are:

1. Employee resistance to change.

2. Lack of management support.

3. Lack of project management and transformation assistance tools such as:

Planning

* Uncontrollable or confused planning.
* Overly optimistic estimates.
* Overloaded resources.
* Too rigid planning.

Organization and coordination

* An inappropriate structure.
* Poorly defined responsibilities.
* Key resources not available.
* A disengagement of functional managers.
* Inappropriate communication.

Execution

- ✳ Projects discontinued along the way.
- ✳ Uncontrolled changes.
- ✳ Poorly estimated complexity.
- ✳ Unbalanced goals.
- ✳ Lack of training.
- ✳ A well-documented project but not followed by concrete actions.

Piloting

- ✳ A lack of authority from the program manager who must oversee the smooth running and progress of all projects.
- ✳ Poor communication and coordination.
- ✳ An inconsistency between current projects.
- ✳ Lack of corrective actions.

Stages of change

— The first step is to build-up a framework

The sponsor

Any change program begins with a clearly defined strategy. We then look at the current situation and make a list of all the projects to be done and all the steps to take to reach the finish line.

The absolute rule for successful change management is the unconditional involvement of the CEO! I have often seen around me that when it comes to implementing IT projects, some CEOs delegate to IT management. This is a big mistake because an IT project must reflect the needs of a new strategy and a new organization of the company. The person who is in the best position to answer questions is therefore unavoidably the CEO.

Their role:

- ✳ Be responsible for the overall program.

* Provide strategic advice.
* Arbitrate in the event of inconsistency or major priority conflict.

The steering committee

Most companies don't always have the resources to invest in their future - they focus on the present. Indeed, it is the daily operations that generate the profits. The challenge is therefore to work for the future while safeguarding the present.

This is why I suggest you set up a steering committee alongside the management committee, which will function normally and pursue its agenda as usual. The steering committee will meet at other times and may be composed of other members (senior executives) depending on the topics discussed.

Its role:

* Validate the project portfolio.
* Monitor the smooth running of projects.
* Decide on operational orientations and accommodations to be made.
* Examine and validate the main achievements of the various projects.
* Make decisions.
* Decide on the next steps and actions.

The program manager

I have noticed in the different companies where I have worked that if there is no one responsible for the change management agenda, things do not move forward and can go wrong.

You have to imagine that an executive who has accepted the responsibility of bringing a project to completion is often not prepared for it. So they need someone to hold their hand and guide them. The program manager must ensure that the presentations that will be made to the steering committee are structured and comprehensive.

I suggest you take an outsider who is experienced. Their job needn't be full time. Depending on the size of your business and the projects, one day a week could be enough.

Their role would be:

* Encourage and coordinate.
* Orchestrate the successful delivery of projects (timing and objectives).
* Follow the progress of projects by being in close contact with their managers.
* Organize and systematize the reporting as well as the preparations for the steering committee.
* Facilitate communication and the mobilization of troops.

The project manager

All projects must have a single manager. We call them the project manager. Their main quality should not be an expert in the field of their project but to manage a team and keep their commitments in terms of timing. They must therefore be structured, credible, and results-oriented. Their major constraint will be to combine their everyday work with the management of their project.

Their role:

* Be in charge of their project.
* Make proposals to the steering committee.
* Follow the project progress.

In short: the objective of change management is intangible, but the means can evolve along the way.

The most important thing for the CEO is to understand that for the majority of project managers, this is their first adventure into the unknown; motivating and listening to them will be the key to success!

— The second step is to choose the right people

In order for your change management to be successful, you must move your teams out of their hierarchy and their usual environment. This is why the choice of executives and employees must be made at the highest level in order to avoid outdated decisions. You implement a missile type structure "parallel" to your current organization.

Take your staff list and indicate behind each name a level 1, 2 or 3.

* **Level 1**: a manager capable of leading a project from A-Z. They do not necessarily have to be an expert on the subject of the project itself.

* **Level 2**: a manager or employee with expertise in the field of the project who can deliver something on their own.

* **Level 3**: someone who can make a specific contribution but who is not in a position to take responsibility on the subject. For example: the skilled worker who knows their tools like the back of their hand. If we forget to ask them their opinion, your whole project may fail.

— The third step will be the implementation of management tools

Many of you have already been confronted with classic project management tools. You will find a plethora of them on the Internet. So, I'm not going to dwell too much on the classic tools. However, I will talk about some of the tools that I have myself put in place that will facilitate the smooth running of your change program. I'll give you three basic tips.

The project list

The first thing to do is to list in an Excel table all the projects that you consider necessary for your organization to be in phase with your strategic plan in the coming months or years. The projects can be of any nature: human resources, sales, marketing, production, R&D, logistics, finance, reporting, IT, suppliers, etc.

You will very amass a list of 20 or even 50 projects. This is where the problems begin. How to decide on the priorities? You will have easy projects which can be "quick wins" and others which are tedious and expensive.

First tip: put a score with colors: one letter = green, two letters = orange, three letters = red.

S Not strategic	SS Strategic	SSS Very strategic
I Not important	II Important	III Very important
U Not urgent	UU Urgent	UUU Very urgent
D Not difficult	DD Difficult	DDD Very difficult
C Not costly	CC Costly	CCC Very costly
T Less than 3 months	TT 3-6 months	TTT Minimum 6 months

Once you have done this exercise, you will immediately see from the colors which projects are easy, inexpensive and at a glance the others which are very strategic, very expensive, very difficult and will take time. Depending on your objectives, your resources and your means, it will be easier for you to make a choice on the first projects that you are going to start.

Example:

ICT migration	SSS	III	U	DDD	CCC	TTT
New showroom	S	III	UUU	D	C	T

Team occupation

For each project that you have chosen, you will need to appoint a project manager. In turn, they will have to name their team. They will have a small stable team and for some sub-projects, they will add names according to the skills required.

Second tip: you will quickly notice that for a large part of your projects, it is always the same names that appear. Force yourself, in agreement with the project manager, to estimate the time needed per week for each person who takes part in a project. Allow at least half a day per week.

List your projects and the names of your employees as well as the time spent by each per project:

Name	Days/week	Project 1	Project 2	Project 3	Project 4	Etc.
John	2,5 days	0,5	0,5	0,75	0,75	
Bill	2,0 days	0,5	1,0	/	0,5	
Olivia	1,0 day	0,5	/	0,5	/	
Emma	1/2 day	/	0,5	/	/	
Etc.						

You immediately see that there is a problem with John because it's impossible for him to leave his daily tasks for more than three half-days a week and he is asked for five. In fact, he is the factory manager, and his repeated absences could affect production. You will therefore have to choose which project will be postponed so that your current business can continue to operate.

The ideal week

Personally, I have always had difficulty mentally retaining scheduled meetings once every three weeks or every second Tuesday of the month. I am sure I am not alone. The human brain tends to remember only a single moment in a standard week. For example: I have my workout scheduled every Wednesday evening and Saturday morning. I assure you; I never forget it. The same thing is valid for planning project teams' meetings. If a manager decides that the meetings will be held every Tuesday afternoon, not only will their project team remember it, but colleagues at work will also remember the date.

* Where's John?
* Well, it's Tuesday afternoon today, he's working with his team on his project.

Third tip: encourage all your project teams to organize themselves into a standard week. This will make life easier for everyone.

The project files

Naming a project is easy. On the other hand, describing it in detail and the goals you want to achieve is much less obvious.

It is nevertheless an essential exercise to make sure that everyone understands the same thing. The number of projects that were abandoned because there was a lack of clarity from the start are legion.

You will easily find several types of project sheets on the Internet. In summary, a project file should contain the following:

* Description of the project.
* A list of members.
* The objectives to be achieved.
* A list of sub-projects with their start and end date.
* The possible risks.
* The cost of the project.
* Signatures from the project manager, the program manager and the sponsor (CEO) to make sure everyone has understood the same thing, and everyone is in agreement with it.

The planning

All the projects will necessarily have to be put in a calendar, to be able to have a view of their overlap but also to take into account holidays, etc.

	Project 1	Project 2	Project 3	Project 4	Project 5
January					
February					
March					
April					
May					
June					
July					
August					
September					
October					
November					
December					

CHAPTER 4
The human aspect in any change management

A company is made up of people. A change management will be successful through the goodwill, motivation, courage and tenacity of its members. But don't be fooled. Every company that goes through a change process will also trigger strong emotions among staff members.

When management announces that there will be changes in your company in order to prepare it for a better future, the majority of staff perceive the message as "danger" and not as "better future." The first word that comes to mind is "restructuring" and not "opportunity". Humans are afraid of the unknown and often imagine the worst.

The first questions could be:

* What's the point? Everything's fine today anyway, right?
* Where are they going to take us?
* What will my role be?
* Will I still have my job?
* Am I able to overcome this change?
* Wasn't it better before?

The main role of the CEO and their management committee will then be to assure, reassure and (re)reassure, and to inspire people to dream. It goes without saying that their message must be sincere because if not, people feel it immediately.

Another action you can take is to quickly identify open-minded individuals within your staff in order to motivate them to join the change movement.

A third topic that matters is using a unifying slogan. At AMP, we called our project "On the Move" and at Fountain "On the Road".

In the following pages, I will tell you about different themes encountered during a change process, which are related to human aspects.

The involvement of managers and employees in the change process

The biggest mistake you could make is to believe that a change process can only be carried out by external consultants. Of course they may have specific skills that are lacking in your company, but they can never replace your managers and employees. Personally, I have a great deal of respect for the consultants I have worked with and some have even become friends. They helped me think out of the box and operated as my sounding board. They also brought me best practice working methods.

If you are faced with a change process, I strongly advise you to call external consultants to help you steer, structure and give rhythm to your change program.

On the other hand, do not substitute them for your executives and employees, for two main reasons:

1. Your executives and employees are the only ones who have in-depth knowledge of your business. They just aren't always used to presenting their work in a structured way. This is where the role of the external consultant will have its added value. They will force your internal teams to ask themselves the right questions and they will help them clarify a problem in all its aspects and consequences. They will then support them to prepare a clear and structured presentation for your steering committee.

2. The consultants leave, your teams stay. What has always frustrated me was having brilliant consultants around for a few weeks or a few months, but when they left, they left only beautiful binders filled with hundreds of charts that no one would look at afterwards. So, it's up to you to make sure that your teams stay in control at all times and that they don't succumb to the temptation of having things done by outside people. Consultants are there to guide you, to help you, but they are not there to replace your managers and employees.

The importance of spreading the spirit of change within the company

Generally, humans do not like change. They prefer to stay in their comfort zone. However, there will be people in your teams who, for personal reasons, will see change as an opportunity for them. I am thinking in particular of all the young executives who feel blocked in their initiatives by their direct boss.

So, don't hesitate at your kick-off meeting! Ask audience members who are interested in one way or another to come forward to be actors of change. You will sometimes be surprised at their enthusiasm.

I like the rule of 1% which becomes 10% and then becomes 100%. The 1% is your Board of Directors and your executive committee who are in line with your strategic plan and its roadmap. Then come the executives and employees who will be part of the project teams. They are the 10%. By the success of their first projects and by their enthusiasm, they will gradually bring with them the other members of your company in the hope that one day 100% of your staff will be part of this positive spirit of change.

In all the companies where I had to lead a change management process, I paid a lot of attention to communication. In order to make sure that critics (they are everywhere) do not spread negative vibes, I set up news bulletins. These bulletins went out every fortnight and talked about current projects with interviews and lots of photos. Sometimes we even sent them to the private addresses of our staff so that their families could also be informed. Believe me, it works!

Change management and chaos

It is better to move forward in disorder than to remain at an organized standstill

As CEO, in times of change, there have been several frustrating situations for me. In the beginning, companies tend to run worse. Habits are broken, people are lost, and some make more mistakes than before. All the daily dissatisfaction obviously gives food for thought to detractors. Why didn't you just leave everything as it was before? Was it right to change this or that?

The comment I have been giving to these people for years is the story of the watch.

You have a fine mechanical watch. It is beautiful and it runs on time. There is only one small problem, it runs backwards. To make it run correctly, you have to take it apart and put it back together. A mechanical watch can have up to a thousand parts. Imagine a table where all these pieces are placed next to each other before they are put together piece by piece in the correct way. Well, it's the same with a business going through a change process. Some will see above all the chaos represented by these pieces arranged on the table while others will have in mind the beautiful watch that's in the making.

Your role as CEO will always be to explain and reassure. So be more than ever physically present in your company, in offices, factories, and logistics depots. Ask workers and employees how they feel. You will then enter into emotional communication to which you will have to respond with great tact and respect. At least everyone will see that you are listening to them and respect them. This will help them get through these difficult changing times.

The change process and the workload

Do not kid yourselves. Any change in a company entails significant additional workload for managers who already have the responsibility of carrying out their own change projects.

Often, the executives chosen to be project managers are already very busy in their current work. I piloted four transition programs in my career and what struck me the most was that these same managers, who were already busy with their day-to-day tasks, were able to find the necessary time to complete their projects.

Initially, during my first change program, I naively thought that my executives and employees would see project management as an extra job. Well, no, not at all. The same thing also happened in the other three companies.

For the vast majority of them, it was an honour to personally contribute to the future of their company. Many of them spent whole evenings and weekends thinking about new modes of organization, new processes, new tools, etc. I still have great admiration for these men and women who offered their time and energy for the good of their company. Those who read this book will recognize themselves.

It is therefore important that any CEO be grateful for this extra work which is not related to any financial recognition. So, here's a little advice. Regularly invite your teams involved in change projects to dine together in a restaurant. This creates a real team spirit and allows its members to feel recognized.

Change management breaks silos

Most of the companies I have known tended to work in silos. Each division, each department worked vertically and did not spontaneously talk to colleagues from other departments. Of course everyone sees each other at the coffee machine, and everyone talks about their weekend, their vacation, but no one ever thinks of talking about work. Since I have been working as a consultant, I've seen this in several companies. It is probably due to cultural history.

However, the specificity of a change program is to compose multidisciplinary teams. The vast majority of change-related projects have a commercial, marketing, R&D, industrial and financial aspect. It is therefore a blessing for colleagues to work on real tasks together when they only knew each other through the company restaurant or the coffee machine. This is how corporate culture changes and becomes more open and therefore more efficient. Never forget to make sure to choose people from different departments when you build project teams.

Respect your employees

During my first change program at AMP, I was still quite young and what mattered most to me was success at all cost. I did not always understand the reluctance of some staff members and saw their attitude as negative without looking any further.

Many years later, during my psychology seminars in Germany, listening to the experiences of several people, I realized that I was completely wrong on the subject. For my part, having moved many times and changed jobs several times, change had become something natural for me.

On the other hand, I had not realized that certain loyal employees who had joined their company at the end of their studies and who had never changed jobs in the last 10 or 20 years, would experience the change as a trauma. Suddenly, as part of a reorganization, they were asked to move to another place and received new tasks to perform. I only realize now why there had been unexplained illnesses.

If you are a young CEO, I ask you (and I know now what I am talking about) to have compassion and respect for those loyal employees and workers who do not understand what is happening to them.

If, at the time, I had spent only a few minutes listening to their dismay, futile to me but important to them, I could have avoided unnecessary suffering.

It is therefore important that communication go both ways in this kind of situation. The quickest route is not always the most successful. Looking back on things, I realize it was not that important to move these people. Looking more closely, we might have found an equivalent solution and could have worked around another way to obtain the same results.

The benefits for your career to work for a company in transition

When you're young and ambitious, you want to move forward. If that's not possible in your company, you leave and go elsewhere. This is often the case when you find yourself stuck in a company where the positions that might be of interest to you are filled and not readily available.

The big advantage when a company decides to revise its strategy and launches a major change program, is that jobs are reshuffled.

This is a fantastic opportunity for very competent executives who are hidden in the maze of an organization.

Some years ago, I had an interim management assignment for a European construction group. I was in the process of setting up project teams in Liège, one of the group's affiliates. The list of projects had been validated in agreement with the local management. We had already decided who would be the future project managers.

One morning, while walking around one of their warehouses, I saw someone I didn't know who was working in an office container at the top of a staircase. I went upstairs, opened the door and introduced myself.

Little by little, I learned that he was an engineer and that he had worked for more than 10 years as the ground equipment maintenance coordinator at TNT, which has since become FedEx.

As I walked up to my office, I spoke to the local manager about him who then half-heartedly agreed to add his name to the list.

I remember that his presentations and suggestions to the steering meetings were very thoughtful and structured. Six months after my first visit, he was appointed "Business Unit Manager Equipment".

This story is further proof that if you are knowledgeable and ambitious, you can create the opportunity to get noticed at a high level in your company. Don't hesitate to take on assignments that may arise so that you can work on a project that will put you in contact with senior leaders. Don't worry: if you're good, they'll notice you. Go for it and be an actor of your future!

THEME 04

THE COMPANY AND THE FIGURES

Every CEO and his management team deserve to have monitoring tools that are easy to use and understand. They should be usable by as many managers and employees as possible rather than just by financial experts. I know that there are dozens of tracking tools on the market. Below and in the following chapters, I will describe some essential principles that will really allow you to run your business in a simple and efficient way.

CHAPTER 1
Your dashboard

When I was CEO of Fountain, we used the services of Bain & Company. I remember one of their partners Patrick D. telling me: *"Pascal, you have to pilot your company as if you were in the cockpit of an airplane. All the important steering components should be found on a single dashboard"*. For me, who used to go every month through dozens of pages to discover my company results, this was really eye-opening advice. So, with my management team, we first built a prototype and after a few months the tool was ready.

Since then, every time I ran a new business, I put this system in place. Believe me, this is really an essential tool for any CEO who wants to run his business because, when used every month, it allows you to pinpoint specific problems that you quickly correct.

What should a dashboard contain?

A dashboard must obviously contain accounting figures but the most important is that this dashboard also includes non-accounting figures that contribute to the success of YOUR business.

In other words, it must also give you information on the performance of your sales network, your industrial and logistics performance, your stock rotation, and elements related to quality, etc.

If you keep track of and therefore improve all the elements on your dashboard, you will quickly improve your cash position as well as your profit. The important thing is that this dashboard comes out every month in order to react timely where necessary!

If your company has several subsidiaries, each one fills in this dashboard and the head office then builds a consolidated report. Over time, you can add the YTD (year to date) as well as the 12 rolling months, in order to compare your monthly performance over time. There is also nothing to prevent you from comparing all of these elements to a given monthly goal.

You will find below a chart that includes the four important areas that a dashboard should include:

1. REVENUES

2. OPERATIONS

3. MARGINS & CASH

4. QUALITY

— REVENUES

This area contains all the elements related to the income of your company as well as those which may contribute to it in the future. This includes revenue, average revenue per customer, number of new customers, number of lost customers, number of new orders, ongoing potential business, backlog, number of offers sent, number of customer visits, conversion rate of your website, etc.

— OPERATIONS

This area contains all the elements related to the operations of your company. If you have a production unit, it is important to define quantified elements that indicate it's efficiency. The same goes for your logistics and the management of your stock of raw materials and finished goods.

Regarding production, this includes the quantity produced (m², volume, etc.), the quantity produced per FTE (full time equivalent), the rate of paid absenteeism, etc.

In terms of logistics, this includes the number of deliveries, revenue per delivery, number of lines per invoice, percentage of transport cost / turnover. Items related to inventory include the inventory value of raw materials, the inventory value of finished goods, the turnover rate of the finished goods inventory as well as the percentage of out of stock of finished goods.

— MARGINS & CASH

This area indicates the elements related to the creation of wealth and the monitoring of the cash situation. It includes the EBITDA [2], the current cash position, the 3-month cash forecast, the average gross margin, the average contribution margin [3], the aging balance, the amount of total trade receivables as well as the DSO [4].

— QUALITY

One thing that is rarely discussed in our Board of Directors' meetings and even in executive committees is quality. Most of the time, we don't lose customers because of price issues but because of all kinds of quality issues.

The quality issues to be taken into account are the number of complaints, the percentage of complaints linked to invoices sent, the percentage of complaints linked to the quality of the product delivered, the percentage of complaints linked to timing, the percentage of complaints related to service, the percentage of "other" complaints, the average number of days between the receipt of a complaint and our response to it, and the NPS rate [5].

REVENUES			
	MONTH	**YTD**	**ROLLING**
Turnover			
Average turnover per customer			
Number of new customers			
Number of lost customers			
Number of new orders			
Ongoing potential business			
Backlog			
Number of offers sent			
Number of customer visits			
Conversion rate of your website			
OPERATIONS			
PRODUCTION	**MONTH**	**YTD**	**ROLLING**
Quantity produced (m², volume, etc.)			
Quantity produced per FTE[1]			
% paid absenteeism			
Logistics			
Number of deliveries			
Revenue per delivery			
Number of lines per invoice			
% transport cost / revenue			
Stock			
Stock value raw materials			
Stock value finished goods			
Stock turnover rate of finished products			
% of out of stock finished products			

---

1. **FTE**: *full-time equivalent.*

2. **EBITDA** : *Earnings before interest, taxes, depreciation, and amortization. EBITDA makes it possible to know the wealth creation of companies in order to be able to compare them with each other without having to take into account their capitalization rate or their debt position. A positive EBITDA means that a company is profitable, but does not necessarily has a net profit. On the other hand, a negative EBITDA means that the company is not profitable.*

MARGINS & CASH			
	MONTH	**YTD**	**ROLLING**
EBITDA[2]			
Current cash position			
Forecast cash position in 3 months			
Average gross margin			
Average contribution margin[3]			
Aging balance[6]			
Total receivables			
DSO[4] in number of days			
QUALITY			
	MONTH	**YTD**	**ROLLING**
Number of complaints			
% complaint / invoices sent			
% complaints related to the quality of the delivered product			
% Late arrival related complaints			
% service complaints			
% "other" complaints			
Average number of days of our response to the complaint			
NPS rate[5]			

---

3. **Contribution margin:** *turnover - cost price - variable costs. This margin makes it possible to see the real contribution of a commercial network. The same exercise can be done for the calculation of an offer for which we do not take into account the fixed costs (because we already have them) but only the variable costs in order to calculate its profitability linked to a predefined price.*

4. **DSO** *or Days Sales Outstanding allows you to find out the average number of days between the issuance of an invoice and the receipt of its payment. The formula is as follows: Trade receivables / Turnover (including tax) x 360. Please note, this formula is only valid for a comparison within a country. When you export, VAT is not invoiced, this could somewhat distort the comparison.*

5. **NPS:** *"Net Promoter Score" is the index that measures the satisfaction of a brand, product or service. The NPS is calculated from a specific question about a customer's satisfaction rate. Promoters: score 9 to 10, Passives: score 7 to 8, Detractors: score 0 to 6 To obtain the NPS, the percentage of detractors must be subtracted from the percentage of promoters. For example: if you have 70% Promoters, 15% Passives, and 15% Detractors, the NPS will be +55. The score can vary between +100 and -100. With a score of around 50 or more, you are highly regarded by your customers.*

6. **Aging balance:** *Document that highlights the delays in collections. It summarizes all the customer accounts that have not been settled, and this by seniority increments of 30 days, 60 days, 90 days and more.*

CHAPTER 2

The commercial network and its profitability

How to measure the real profitability of your sales network

Every company has a commercial network. Its success is easy to measure by the revenue achieved in each region or country. However, it is a little more difficult to measure the real contribution of each country to the benefit of your company.

This is why I suggest that you measure your sales network on the contribution margin (3) it brings to the group and not just on its revenue.

Indeed, in order to be profitable, a salesperson must at least generate more margins than costs.

I take for example a country outside the headquarters country, for example Germany. In order to calculate Germany's contribution margin, I take into account the revenue achieved, and I calculate my average gross margin on this revenue. That's the gross amount that goes into my pocket. Then, I deduct from this amount the costs strictly linked to the German network: logistics costs, office rental, the sales reps' salaries as well as their expense accounts, and the cost of local trade shows.

However, I do not take into account the cost of an international fair which takes place in Frankfurt or Cologne. In fact, these shows welcome visitors from all over the world and are therefore within the budget of the group marketing team.

This also applies to the cost of creating a website and creating sales flyers. We could also take into account the cost of translation, but as we often receive an invoice that includes translation into several languages, there is no point.

Example: Calculation of the contribution margin of the sales network in Germany:

Turnover:	**2 000 000 €**
Cost price:	**-1 000 000 €**
Logistics costs:	**-60 000 €**
Cost of office rental:	**-50 000 €**
Cost of sales staff:	**-400 000 €**
Salaries & expenses:	**-100 000 €**
Trade show fees:	**-50 000 €**
CONTRIBUTION MARGIN OF THE SALES NETWORK IN GERMANY:	**340 000 €**

The big advantage of this calculation is that you can measure what each network actually generates for you. Often, we tend not to take all these costs into account because they are embedded in the general accounts such as transport costs, trade show fees and expense reports from salespeople.

What indicators can become false friends?

— Do not confuse turnover and margins

Forecasted revenue is a good indicator, but it is certainly not the only one. In all the companies that I have managed as CEO, I have always paid a lot of attention to margins.

Carrying out a 100,000 $ deal with 20% gross margin or 50% gross margin does not give the same end result. If a salesperson costs you 100,000 $ annually, he will have to generate at least a 100,000 $ in margin. This means that he will have to achieve a turnover of 200,000 $ if the margin is 50% but if it is 20%, he will have to achieve an annual turnover of 500,000 $. I know this calculation is simplistic, but you would be surprised by how many business leaders do not take this data into account enough when measuring the effectiveness of their network and / or their product portfolio.

— When a percentage plays a bad trick on you

I remember a company I joined in 2015 in order to straighten out the situation. The previous management had simply decided to refuse any business with less than a 30% margin. The sales department therefore had to abandon a very large customer in an Eastern European country. The catch was that this historic customer had been buying 3 million euros per year for years. Suddenly, the company lost 600,000 € overnight in profit. Because the company's fixed costs remained the same, this translated into an EBITDA loss of 600,000 €. As soon as I arrived, I did everything to win back this client. Unfortunately, in the meantime they had found another supplier with whom they were very happy. I won't tell you my frustration when I learned this ... As we were purchasing our products in China, this loss of this customer had an impact on our purchase prices which became higher due to a drop in volume.

It is therefore your responsibility as CEO to properly judge all aspects related to your customers' portfolio before making far-reaching and hasty decisions.

— The Importance of a wide range of customers

A phrase that I often hear in corporate corridors: "We have too many small customers, why not just keep the big ones?" Whether you like it or not, the Pareto law, or the 80-20 law, applies in all companies where 20% of customers make 80% of your sales.

Your role is not to let small customers down. Your role is to ensure that they remain profitable by adjusting the level of your service.

When I was managing the Fountain group, listed on Euronext, we had approximately 50,000 customers.

I segmented them according to their size and their annual purchases:

* 5% of customers with more than 20 users annually bought for more than 3,000 € and represented 25% of our revenue.
* 25% of customers with 5 to 20 users annually bought between 1,000 € and 3,000 € and represented 45% of our revenue.
* 70% of customers with less than 5 users annually bought for less than 1,000 € and represented 30% of our revenue.

We generated 20% EBITDA on our revenue.

Each segment had an offer, pricing and service adapted to their size. Each segment had a good margin. Large customers generated a healthy turnover per customer with a lower gross margin in percentage but good in absolute. They were contacted at least every month. Smaller customers had a much lower turnover but had a much larger percentage margin. They were contacted every 3 months.

It was this number and the mix of customers that provided long-term, sustainable advantage over time.

This same exercise can be done in your business. Accept large accounts with low margins but also care for your small clients as long as they have a good margin. Little streams make big rivers.

CHAPTER 3

The profit calculation and the importance of cash

How to easily define your public price while ensuring your gross margin

I'll give you a concrete example that I used a few years ago in a commercial (non-industrial) company. Our range included approximately 250 SKU's (unique product references). The difficulty was to define the correct public price including tax for each of these products while achieving an approximate gross margin[1] of 55%.

If our landed cost was 100 €, the public selling price had to be 400 € including tax. So, we had to have a factor of 4.

Here is the calculation :

Landed cost	100 €
Selling price with 55% margin	222 €
33% distributor's margin	332 €
Public price (21% inc. VAT)	**401 €**

---

1. *Gross Margin = Selling price - landed cost price (purchase price + transport price + import duties).*

I advise you to always find a way to simplify things. Always try to find a calculation solution that everyone can understand.

Our sales manager for France had given us information on prices, volume and product characteristics that major distributors in France would be ready to purchase if we met their demand. When I was in China with my purchasing manager, it was easy for us to negotiate prices with our contacts using this factor. We knew very quickly whether their final price was acceptable or not.

How to calculate your gross margin in an industrial company

It is easy to calculate the gross margin in a trading company. Making this same calculation in an industrial company is much more difficult. In fact, you have a production tool that involves significant investments and fixed costs. The gross margin is then calculated as follows:

Gross Margin = Selling price - Cost price[1]

As for your raw material costs, it is quite easy. However, your different production units have very different returns from one period to the next due to machine stoppages, accidents, absenteeism and other factors. This means that the cost of manufacturing the same product can vary from batch to batch.

I advise you to work with a standard costing such as the theoretical number of hours of preparation, production, finishing by the staff as well as the cost of machine time. You know the hourly cost of your workers. By adding an average absenteeism rate, you can calculate very precisely the theoretical cost of their time spent per task.

For the hourly cost of the machines, it is a bit more complicated. Just because a machine is depreciated does not mean that it costs nothing. You therefore need to know its replacement cost, its lifespan as well as its energy consumption and spare parts needed. Once you have all that information,

---

1. *Cost price: Includes all the costs of producing goods for a company. It includes the purchase price of raw materials, consumables and supplies, as well as the cost of labour, machine depreciation, and in general every cost necessary for production.*

you can calculate its annual average cost. You divide that cost by the number of hours it is theoretically used per year in order to obtain its standard hourly cost. Then you multiply the standard hourly cost by the actual number of hours the machine has been used.

To calculate the price of your product, you then use your standard cost price.

On the other hand, for your plant manager, it is important to measure the variance between the standard cost and the reality in the field. This will be a weekly discussion topic with their team, and it will be a way to continuously optimize their production tool and thus improve your margins. In their variance analysis, they must take into account several elements, in particular if the variance is due to a machine failure or to higher consumption. Based on these variances, they will adapt standard costs where necessary.

Having done this exercise myself with Excel in the last company I managed, I can assure you that it allowed us to make dozens of offers in record time with very precise calculated margins.

Why is cash key to any business?

Cash can be simultaneously a fantastic lever for a company, but it can also very quickly become its worst enemy when it is borrowed.

With the cost of money near zero in 2021, many companies consider the risks to be minimal when borrowing money. Effectively injecting 20% of your own money and borrowing 80% at low cost can be tempting when the company is making big profits after a few years.

Your professional life can sometimes give you surprises. Who would have thought in 2019 that in 2020 we would have the worst crisis of the century because of COVID-19?

My advice is therefore to always have reserves or the possibility of short-term credit in a bank, just in case...

Which companies are structurally the most affected by cash problems? Fast-growing companies such as start-ups. Indeed, from day one, you have operating costs but no customers yet. Then when your company starts to grow, you have to finance your goods and your production equipment before you are even paid by your customers. The stronger your growth, the more cash you burn because your customers will pay you after you have paid your suppliers and staff. The notion of working capital requirement[1] is therefore necessary to consider when making a business plan.

Paradoxically, the opposite happens when your turnover drops. Indeed, your 30-day or 60-day invoices are paid but your order book is declining. You therefore have fewer bills to pay to your suppliers and therefore your cash levels can rise.

Let's not talk about misfortune

You have no idea how many businesses large and small that at first glance had no apparent problems but went into bankruptcy or came close to it. The main reason was that their CEO was putting all his energy into internal and external growth without worrying about whether his company had a financial backbone strong enough to support it. At some point, you'll find that you don't have enough money to pay your monthly bills. At first, you start paying your bills with some delay. Then, you only pay the suppliers who are complaining. And then comes the day when it may well prove to be the straw that breaks the camel's back. A big supplier will refuse to deliver your merchandise, you no longer honour your agreements (covenants) with your bank, and then everything will go downhill to a possible bankruptcy.

Why is following the DSO almost more important than following the aging balance?

It is important for any CEO to ensure that customers pay on time and that an organization is in place to call customers who are late in paying their bills. To ensure follow-up, the accounting department uses the aging balance. The flaw of this tool is that it only mentions if a customer has an outstanding amount with respect to a given date. The DSO (days sales outstanding) (4), on

---

1. *The working capital requirement: The amount that a company must finance to cover the need resulting from cash flow gaps between inflows and outflows. Calculation WCR = Open customer invoices + stocks - invoices payable to suppliers.*

the other hand, gives you the average number of days between the issuance of an invoice and its payment.

When I was CEO of Fountain, I noticed that my Parisian subsidiary was always running low on cash, unlike my subsidiary in Nantes, which had an excess of cash. Both subsidiaries had aging balances of equivalent quality. However, the DSO in Nantes was 28 days while in Paris it was 60 days. After an audit, I noticed that some smart kids sometimes changed the terms of payment of some late-paying customers so that they no longer appeared on the aging balance (6). I can tell you that I quickly took the necessary measures and that employees had to leave the company immediately.

CHAPTER 4

Quality and customer satisfaction

Quality is the CEO's business!

Do not think that responsibility for quality should be given to someone or to a department. To delegate quality to a department denies that quality is everyone's business. You will understand, I am against the appointment of a quality manager. It's so easy for the rest of the company to say, *"It's not my problem, it's theirs".*

If a manager is to be appointed for quality, it should be the CEO. Why? Quality is a generic term, but it encapsulates so many aspects that it affects all departments of your company.

Let's start from the beginning. Who is the first to realize that there is a quality problem? It's the customer, of course. Who is the first victim of a lack of quality? It's you, because if you don't manage quality properly, eventually you will lose customers.

The quality problem can take on various aspects. So, it can be...

* **Commercial**
  The salesperson sold a product to a customer that does not correspond to reality or they committed to a deadline that they knew to be untenable.

* **Administrative**
  An order was incorrectly encoded. An invoice was incorrectly worded. The price was not the one specified on the order form, etc.

* **Logistics**

  It often happens that problems are related to the carrier. The goods are damaged on arrival and the customer has not made an immediate complaint.

* **Qualitative**

  The quality of the product may not keep its promise of robustness over time or, more typically, it may have fallen through the cracks of quality control at the production stage.

The CEO's responsibility is to verify that all complaints are processed, that a register is created, that the requests are handled by the appropriate department and that, even if a quick solution is not found, the customer is informed that his complaint has been taken into consideration.

The topic "complaints and quality" should be part of the agenda in all management meetings. There is no need to go into detail, but each complaint should activate a "call-to-action" in the company so that people can improve the way they work.

What is NPS and what is it for?

The NPS[1] (Net Promoter Score) is a customer satisfaction measurement tool that is used by most large multinationals (see examples in the graph below).

If the score is 9 or 10, he becomes "*Promoter*".

If the score is 7 or 8, it is "*Passive*".

If the score is between 0 to 6, he becomes "*Detractor*".

To obtain the NPS, subtract the percentage of Detractors from the percentage of Promoters. For example: if you have 70% Promoters, 15% Passives, and 15% Detractors, the NPS will be +55. The score can vary from +100 to -100. With a score of around 50 or more, you are highly regarded by your customers.

---

1. *NPS: "Net Promoter Score" is the index that measures the satisfaction of a brand, product or service. The NPS is calculated from a specific question about a customer's satisfaction level.*

Here are some examples of NPS scores in 2020:

NPS score 2020	
77	Starbucks
67	Samsung
47	Apple
45	Coolblue
40	BMW
28	Adidas
25	Amazon
14	Disney
-8	McDonald's
-9	IKEA
-21	Facebook
SOURCE : CUSTOMER.GURU	

I personally met with the CEO of Coolblue and several of its employees. It's a Dutch company and No. 2 in online sales in Belgium after Amazon. All their staff are measured against the group's NPS results.

I therefore strongly suggest that you consider installing an NPS survey system in your company and regularly post its results on its billboards. This is when the phrase "customer centricity" takes on its full meaning.

How do customer satisfaction and your company's image go hand in hand?

You will have understood that for me the image of the company is closely linked to quality and customer satisfaction. It must also be a state of mind that permeates the mindset of all employees.

Often, companies invest fortunes to achieve rapid growth without thinking about verifying that the quality of their products or services meet market standards.

If you want to build a sustainable company with good margins and with constant growth, you can only be successful if you continuously check on your customer's satisfaction. For this, your company must have operational excellence as a primary objective.

The only way to do this is to collect constant feedback from your customers and to react quickly. The icing on the cake is that the price of your product or service will no longer be the main criteria on which the customer will decide to trade with you.

Epilogue

Sharing my personal and human experience with you, as well as my professional life, has been a challenge that I would never have accomplished on my own.

For years, I have dreamed of sharing my experience of what "the seven lives" of a CEO have been like. Finally, I thought to myself: Why not use the same methods for writing a book that I have used throughout my professional life?

So, I handled writing this book as a business venture. I took a course to learn to write. I then surrounded myself with competent people with a common vision and values for the proofreading, translation, layout and the launch of my book.

You will probably have noticed throughout the book: a CEO is alone.

They are advised but they alone make the decisions. It's up to them to pull the plough, inspire, and motivate their troops. They are the one to turn to when problems need to be solved and solutions need to be found.

Finally, it is up to them to surround themselves with the right people who share the same values and to use the right tools that will help them run their business.

Since I've become a consultant, I've had real pleasure helping companies grow, build new visions for the future, structure themselves and change dimension in order to succeed in their transition from SMEs to larger companies.

Indeed, this transition requires the effort to let go, surround yourself well, delegate and trust. This choice also implies having IT and management tools that can manage growing complexity.

I admire those entrepreneurs who started their businesses from an idea and who, through their energy, persuasion and stamina, succeeded after a few years in having a successful business. In some cases, I joined their business after it was sold in order to give it a boost.

My years spent as CEO of such diverse companies, both in their business area and in their size, have enabled me to use the right reflexes and to make very quick and accurate diagnosis.

I hope that by reading this book and with this little bonus it will help you to succeed in your business.

Good luck to you!

About the Author

Pascal Wuillaume, advisor to business leaders, structuring agent, international speaker, was born and raised in Ghent, in the north of Belgium, to a French-speaking family. He holds a master's degree in Applied Economics from the University of Antwerp and an MBA from the Stern School of Business at New York University.

As a child, he always dreamed of being a world citizen. This dream came true when he joined a French IT multinational.

He began in France, then was quickly offered an opportunity in New York. In 1990, in the same company, he was promoted to the position of Managing Director of Bull Far East, based in Singapore. It was in 1995, after 13 years abroad, that he finally returned to Belgium.

This international experience taught him three principles that are still anchored in his dynamics:

1. Being a pioneer in the use of digital technologies allows you to be more efficient in your tasks.

2. Learning how to work in a rapidly changing world is paramount.

3. Taking into account cultural specificities within international companies is essential for constructive collaborations.

His 25 years of experience as CEO for various international, family and listed groups have enabled him to quickly diagnose the essential problems to be solved in order to make them sustainable.

In all the companies he has had the chance to lead, it has always been essential for him to energize the teams, to help them look to the future and to combine the resources of different departments in order to create synergies that stimulate the work on joint projects.

Since 2005, he has been a professor in the MBA program of the Solvay Brussels School of Economics and Management in Vietnam. He teaches "Managing the Future".

Having become a consultant in 2020, he supports top executives through the major phases of their company's transformation: accelerated growth, internationalization, transmission and integration after merger.

www.ingramcontent.com/pod-product-compliance
Lightning Source LLC
Chambersburg PA
CBHW070331220526
45467CB00001B/118